Christine Brückner, author of twenty-five books, is one of Germany's most eminent novelists and writers of short stories, plays, children's books and journalism. She lives in Kassel.

After graduating from Cambridge in Modern Languages, the actress and writer Eleanor Bron first became known in the 1960s in satirical cabaret. She went on to become equally admired as a dramatic actress in films, television and on the stage. She has been a contributor to the BBC series 'Words' and 'More Words' and to the book of essays *My Cambridge*. With co-author John Fortune she wrote the book *Is Your Marriage Really Necessary?* Her other autobiographical works are *Life and Other Punctures* and *The Pillow Book of Eleanor Bron or An Actress Despairs*. *Desdemona — if you had only spoken!* is her first published translation.

# *Desdemona – if you had only spoken!*

## Eleven uncensored speeches of eleven incensed women

By

# Christine Brückner

Presented and translated by

# Eleanor Bron

05401240

Published by VIRAGO PRESS Limited 1992
20–23 Mandela Street, Camden Town, London NW1 0HQ

First published in Germany by Hoffmann und Campe Verlag
as *Wenn du geredet hättest, Desdemona*, 1983

*A CIP catalogue record for this book is available from the British
Library*

All rights whatsoever in this work are strictly reserved
and any application for performance must be made in advance
before the beginning of rehearsal to Rosica Colin Limited,
1 Clareville Grove Mews, London SW7 5AH (on behalf of Stefani Hunzinger)
for Christine Brückner, and to Faith Evans, 5 Dryden Street,
Covent Garden, London WC2N 9NW for Eleanor Bron.

Typeset by Falcon Typographic Art Ltd, Fife, Scotland
Printed in Great Britain by Cox & Wyman Ltd, Reading Beckshire

# Contents

# Foreword by Eleanor Bron

February 1992

Dear Reader,

Coming now to the end of these my labours in translating Christine Brückner's monologues, and here the publishers have asked me to write a foreword, introduce them — how did I come across them, why did they appeal to me, my first go at translating, the adaptation and performance of four of the speeches for a one-woman show — anything and everything about the book and me. They think that in Britain people who might know my name but not Christine Brückner's, and who may even have bought the book for that reason, will be interested by these sidelights on my experience and in particular on my experience of experiencing the work they are about to read. I hope that is so. It feels odd; because although I didn't know Frau Brückner's work before, she is so very well-known in her own country — for her novels, children's books, essays, newspaper columns, for her observations on contemporary life.

I have to admit that I don't much like forewords myself. When I do read them I prefer it to be after, not before, I have read the book of the title, so that — I delude myself — I come to the text in something like innocence, without having had my mind tugged or tilted by nibbling at the little old apple up there on its tree. If I were you — as I most often am — one of the much-maligned public, having skimmed the book, weighed up its size and internal shapes, sampled a few sentences, and then completed that delicious transaction which is like actually purchasing hope and the promise of ecstasy, I'd already be in there, at the bus-stop, or on the escalator,* wallowing in among the pages and insights and manifold richness that Frau Brückner offers. If, in addition, what I say can be of interest or profit to anyone at all, be it only to promote the abolition of forewords, then I am happy to say on, and tell all. The value of the book will remain where it should be, in the eleven unspoken speeches of irate and underrated women, disaffected dames, appalled appendages . . . The subtitle already gave me a hint of the many forms of translator's twitch that lay ahead. How to convey its ingenious pun? Literally it means speeches that have never been made, never been outside of these women who are beside themselves . . . I settled for: 'Eleven uncensored speeches of eleven incensed women'.

Any reader whose pattern of book-reading is like mine and who is therefore happy to eat the omelette before the soup, will know that by writing this letter to you I am only following in Christine Brückner's footsteps, pursuing that sincere (but dispiriting) form of flattery which is imitation. One of the pieces takes the form of a letter by the author to a nineteenth-century feminist, with the striking name of Fraülein Malvida von Meysenbug, and to her Frau Brückner speaks in her own voice, a stabilising sound that offsets the ten other voices that she has conjured out of history and legend. I use my voice here not to offset anything at all, but chiefly to eschew the

---

* Well – I'm usually on a bike, so I'd have to wait until I got home to my kitchen stool and mug of tea. (See *Life and Other Punctures*, André Deutsch 1978.)

academic and offer a more personal account. See! the screen begins to wobble like a jelly . . . I cast back my mind. Two years. To Hamburg . . .

During the interval of a dreary play, a row of photographs in the foyer of a tiny theatre in Hamburg – from some other production – raised my spirits. All of them were of women, and not just any women – almost all were women who were known to me, from history, ancient as well as modern, or from literature; some, such as Desdemona or Mary, Mother of Jesus, were familiar because of their association with a more famous man; others were barely known at all – also because of their association with a famous man, that is to say they were mere wives or lovers; still others were actually famous themselves, but in their lives had been like the ideal Victorian child – glimpsed but not really heard. There was even an anti-heroine, representative of the twentieth century, the terrorist Gudrun Ensslin.

Actresses are always on the lookout for protein-packed parts; more than ever these days. Though we may prefer the immediacy of an offer in the form of a phone call, or a script brought round by a helmeted biker, lately it has been increasingly necessary for us – if I may use a redolent eighties phrase – to get on our bikes and go out looking. The number of thespians goes on growing, but not so the number of jobs; and the proportion of male to female roles, even in commercials, still seems to reflect an unreal situation – as if women were less involved in life than men, their lives of less interest. Perhaps one element of the reality is that, on the contrary, they are *so* involved that, even today, they have less time and fewer opportunities to distance themselves from living, ironing, cooking, cleaning, word-processing, for long enough to write about it; and their conditioning, though shifting now at last, still runs counter to the notion that they could ever be fit commentators on the passing scene.

The photographs in the foyer suggested that somebody somewhere was very much aware of how things are, and have been for too long. They were from a production called: *Wenn du geredet hättest, Desdemona. (Desdemona — if you had only spoken!)*; the author was Christine Brückner. I was at once gripped by the excitement of the possible — the book before you've bought it, the script before you've opened it, the moment of being asked to play a part you want — before all those other moments wrestling with it, which may produce a different, inconstant exhilaration, and may not. The next day, in a bookshop in a street lined with bookshops behind the town hall, I found a copy of the book easily, among a row of books by Christine Brückner, a yellow paperback. It turned out to be not a play, but a collection of imagined speeches by misunderstood or neglected or invisible, bewildered women who had never had the chance to have their say. I found out later that the book was almost a 'sport' in Frau Brückner's work. Though she had written one or two plays for the stage and for radio she had started as a novelist. Born in 1921, the daughter of a pastor, she grew up under the Nazi régime, which for her meant a great deal of upheaval, changing towns and changing jobs. Her dream of becoming an architect was not to be; she took to writing instead. In 1954 her first novel won a prize and since then her output has been prolific. She is an admirer of the novelist Theodor Fontane* and shares with him a lightness of tone and an ability to be ironic and touching. She wrote *Wenn du geredet*

* See page 107 for a few more details about Theodor Fontane.

*hättest, Desdemona* almost as diversion, but evidently touched a chord in her readers, whose response took her by surprise.

German was my second language, at University. (When I was interviewed for a place at Oxford I was told: 'Of course your German isn't as good as your French. And your French isn't really up to standard, is it?' After that I was not surprised – and in the circumstances was rather pleased – when they failed to offer me a place. I was baffled to know why they had bothered to drag me there at all.* They were right about my German.) But in spite of its being so far from excellent, I had been taught at school by a superlative teacher, Eva Paneth. My lack of excellence was no reflection on her, but my love of the language and its literature were. On the trip to Hamburg I had decided I would resurrect the pale remains of my grasp on German, and had taken with me, in one of those slim delicate Insel editions, a novella, which had stood on my shelf for twenty years unread. In the intervening years my German had not undergone any miraculous improvement – it did begin to come back slowly – but my pleasure in the language was still there. So my first reading of *Desdemona – if you had only spoken!* – was tantalising. It gave me gists and gleanings, but the gists were full of holes and misreadings and the gleanings intermittent. Even so, what I read so slowly and haltingly threw me further and further into a state of pleasurable agitation – that powerful blend of nervousness and impatience which is a call to act, as opposed to action. What was clear was that the eleven women lying between the covers of the little yellow book,

* See my chapter in *My Cambridge*, edited and introduced by Ronald Hayman, Robson Books 1977.

would have no trouble stepping out onto a stage – as diverse as they were, in age, in history, in personality, there was one quality at least which they shared, the quality expressed in the subtitle: *Eleven uncensored speeches of eleven incensed women.* All these women had things to say that they had never yet had the chance to say, and they had had enough of their enforced silence: they were all angry. In any rehearsal or acting workshop there is one crucial question which crops up over and over again: *Why* does this person speak now? The answer to the question provides the energy that gives the character life. The entire premise of Christine Brückner's book was each woman's urgent need to speak out, at last, now.

When at first I read the names of the protagonists I assumed that as far as any notion of performing them went, I should have to rule out at least five, those five which were rooted in German literature or history: Goethe's wife, Martin Luther's wife, Effi Briest, Gudrun Ensslin and a woman with the strange name of Fräulein Malvida von Meysenbug. In spite of all my studies I was very ignorant of Goethe's domestic arrangements and it hadn't even occurred to me that Martin Luther might have been married; I knew that Fontane's famous novel *Effi Briest* had been made into a film by Fassbinder in 1974, and had always meant to read it, or at least to try to see the film; I had seen a film about a German woman terrorist and her more conventional sister, and perhaps it had been based on Gudrun Ensslin; I had never heard of Fräulein von Meysenbug. But my assumption that I had to rule these ladies out turned out to be quite wrong. Christine Brückner had set out the facts so that the issues at stake become clear very rapidly; the dramatic moment is carefully chosen. In spite of the great gaps in my knowledge I found myself intrigued and drawn in and on. After reading each piece I was curious to find out more, but my chief difficulties were of vocabulary rather than information – detailed knowledge was not essential to enjoyment of the pieces. Later, when I turned to encyclopaedias to satisfy my curiosity, I found that each woman's history seemed already familiar to me. The author's researches were woven into the fabric of the texts, so that each had a distinct and individual flavour. It may be that for an English audience, reading a translation, a few notes* may be helpful; but part of my own pleasure came from meeting each character without preconceived ideas. Only one of the eleven did I back away from, with a sense of déjà vu, and that was Mary – a role I had played in a film called *The Day That Christ Died*. (Rather a small role, for obvious reasons. I have written elsewhere about the horror of doing reaction shots to a Crucifixion scene that was filmed several days before you arrived at the location . . .) When I overcame my reluctance I found Christine Brückner's Mary was a very different person from the woman I had known, much older, very vulnerable, very bewildered.

But it isn't only the women that we meet here because these women, for the most part, are never simply unburdening themselves to some anonymous abstraction. Each time the

---

* At a translators' conference I attended it came out that publishers are terrified of footnotes because they think they put the public off. I happen to love footnotes, especially ones like this literally at the foot of the page, because they allow for expansion and breaths of air and unexpected insights. I have kept them to a minimum. I hope I am allowed to keep these few wee ones, if only as proof of Virago's mettle.

personality of the speaker's audience is evoked almost as vividly as the speaker herself. Thus Luther emerges, testy, autocratic, unworldly, unrealistic, sweeping all before him, eating non-stop, talking non-stop, taking Katharina for granted. (Though she can defend herself – we don't need to feel sorry for her!) We see Frau von Stein, wife of the Oberstallmeister, one time soul-mate – purely platonic – of Goethe, listening with tight lips, aggravated and outraged, while her unbidden guest, Goethe's low-born wife Christiane, lingers on and on, holding forth about life and love to the last drop of port in the decanter. We see Lysistrata among the shifting, embarrassed throng of upright Athenian women discomfitted by the humorous worldly-wise heckling of the courtesan, Megara. Clytaemnestra can only get Agamemnon's ear when he is dead – by her hand – and about to be buried. She addresses the drop-bellied bully as he lies in state on his bier; Effi, disgraced and cast out from society, addresses her regrets and reflections to her deaf old dog Rollo, who is about as able to hear and understand them as ever her hidebound, insensitive husband Instetten was.

Christine Brückner herself emerges as a feminist but not a separatist, a person who sees and denounces men's faults, but does not want to abolish the entire breed. Her voice, which can be heard throughout, is certainly speaking for women and can be gentle and forceful, witty, sad, perceptive, above all humane. The pleasures of heterosexual sex are rated very high by Christine Brückner's creations, almost without exception. Megara lives by it; Christiane revels in it; Laura bitterly resents having been deprived of it; Desdemona depends on it (and in Christine Brückner's version is saved by it); Katharina, the ex-nun, learned to like it. It is quite a shock when in spite of her reputation even Sappho, surrounded as she is by the young girls she teaches and loves, is found to be pining after Phaon, the ferryman. Only Malvida von Meysenbug, a nineteenth-century feminist, utopian and idealist seems to have opted for sublimation, at least later on in life, and for this Christine Brückner takes her roundly to task. Meysenbug considers that sex without its primary object of child-bearing becomes disgusting, and recommends total abstinence for anyone who is past procreating; this suggestion is greeted with horror and amazement by Frau Brückner: Fräulein von Meysenbug may achieve ecstasy reading Schopenhauer, but that is not Brückner's way.

Brückner's way, as I read her, has great appeal. It is the way of the world – not a fantasy or an ideal world, but the world as it is for a whole lot of people. She compares von Meysenbug's vision of a future filled with enlightenment and prosperity to life in western society today; some of von Meysenbug's dreams have indeed come a little closer to realisation, yet the results are not always ideal. In many modern societies such ideals as can still be found are superficial rather than profound; they have more to do with material goods than with Good itself. What Christine Brückner is against, is any distortion of life by false values – something men and women both experience; but since, after only a few decades of feminism, our society is still chiefly devised by men, it's an experience that women suffer more directly. Men tend to feel the side-effects.

As for these same Men, they emerge from the margins of these pages, fallible human beings rather than monsters. Clytaemnestra could forgive Agamemnon once, when she married him, for the murder of her first husband and children, but not a second time when he was able to bring himself to sacrifice their own daughter Iphigenia. But even through her poisoned eyes she can see how pathetic he is with his pursuit of youth, in the form of nubile slaves, and power. Innstetten, wronged by Effi, is also the victim of his rigid Prussian upbringing, his ambition and his inability to see beyond what society dictates to any profounder values, much less to question what exists.

Well! I find, a little to my surprise, that I could go on in this wise, analysing and expounding like an *explication de texte*, but I won't, because I can feel myself drifting into the very essence of the type of weekly essay that I used so to dread having to write when I was a student, as well as into the sort of foreword that I am so dubious about. Besides, I am told that you will want to know more about what went into the show that I eventually did do – for two performances – getting it on and so on – all of which required a kind of persistence that I don't often muster. That persistence in itself says a lot about the 'material' and the impression it made on me.

A brief parenthesis here to muse on the way these days literary texts are more and more often turned into 'material' – into something that can be shaped and cut, performed and generally re-presented as something else. It is a phenomenon that arouses feelings of guilt in me. I am torn between being glad that good – even mediocre – work can live a longer life and find a wider audience; that some authors dead or alive, have a better chance of earning a crust; and being sad that the transferring to another medium – film, TV, radio – can never be perfect. The fact that it happens so often suggests that we are becoming less able to generate original work. Television, as we know, is an insatiable monster that gobbles virgins without a second thought and is not averse to the odd adulterous matron either. The actress in me, however, is not torn by this dilemma, but, greedy and eager, if not desperate.* So, with my newfound persistence, I pursued the possibility of performing the monologues in some form. Monologues, once the province of after-supper recitation and revue, had recently started to find favour once again. This revival owed a lot to Alan Bennett's television series 'Talking Heads', which resuscitated the form by demonstrating its richness and variety. It also owed a lot to the economic climate, which meant that television drama departments and commercial theatres as well as festivals and community centres were looking for low-budget shows. They still are. Including a one-person show in a repertory season might make it possible to have fifteen people in the Christmas panto. In reality, a one-person show is usually very far from being a one-person show, but in terms of finance it is still a case where 'less is less', and in its initial stages at least, it can be worked on by a lone out-of-work actor.

Back in England, once I had read the book, I wrote to the author at her home in Kassel, and very soon received a friendly reply, which was encouraging, but naturally referred me to her agent. It turned out that one or two of the pieces had been translated and were being recorded for Radio 3. They were kind enough to send them to me. But I glanced at the first lines and put the pages away: I already knew that if it were at all possible I wanted to have a go at translating them myself, for myself, and I wanted to keep myself pure. I wasn't confident that it was a job I could even approach.

* See *The Pillow Book of Eleanor Bron or An Actress Despairs*, Methuen, 1987.

I did know that it was essential to have at least one other eye on what I did. There are boundless stories telling how even the most experienced translators miss or mistranslate the odd point, and I didn't expect to be any exception. Dr John Rignall, Lecturer in the English Department at Warwick University agreed to be an eye, and was a marvel of sympathetic patience when confronted by my system, which offered him rows of alternative words and phrases, separated by a slash. (My natural reluctance to commit myself came into its own with this new craft; translating provides the ideal element for a ditherer.)

Here it was a question not only of what was correct as regards style and meaning and tone, but of how it would 'say' — what would it be like speaking these words, how would this character express herself in English? Spoken English uses more words than the written language. Economy and a certain kind of stylish nicety can seem stilted and literary. I tried to hear the voice of each speaker. Gudrun, apart from being foul-mouthed had also been a teacher and from time to time had a touch of the pedant; Effi still retained a simplicity and a childishness, and a child's way of stringing a lot of ideas together using 'and'. Eva Paneth, my first mentor in German, pointed out that I wasn't giving enough force to the little particle 'doch', which is — like 'si' in French — 'an affirmation in response to an implied negative', I looked through the entire text to remedy this fault, and was startled and moved to find that Effi, who feels the whole world turned against her, uses 'doch' in almost every other sentence, trying to put her case in the hearing she has never been allowed. Occasionally the choosing of one word gave me an unexpected perception of the whole character — trying to find the best way to translate the German word *hell*, which can mean both 'light' and 'clever', I suddenly thought that 'canny' hit it about right and that what was more Katharina Luther, ex-nun, might well speak in the down-to-earth Presbyterian tones of a sober Scotswoman. Christiane von Goethe is wounded when she learns that – because of her love of the open air and unfashionably tanned complexion – gossip has spitefully portrayed her as 'a black pudding gone berserk'. The black pudding completed my sense of her as a northern lass, and suggested employing the northern use of 'us' instead of 'we' as an equivalent for Christiane's sometimes unorthodox syntax. I learned to compromise – because you can get close some of the time but not all – and to cheat too and be impure. *Kloster* looks as if it means cloister, but actually means either a monastery or a convent, depending on the context. But to me 'You in your monastery and me in my convent' doesn't say as well, or sound as close to *du in deinem Kloster, ich in dem meinen*, as 'You in your cloister and me in mine'. And of course there are huge stumbling blocks as you try to cross from one language to another. In everyday life Germans still say 'thou' and 'thee' and 'thine' to one another, and to God; but to say that today in English transports you into Archadia and gives a falsely historical feel. Katharina drifts in and out of the second person when she speaks to Luther, Mary uses it exclusively when she calls upon God. Without it you lose intimacy and accuracy, but gain – I hope – immediacy.

With my new interest and persona I recently attended a translator's conference* – on the subject of translating from and into French – and was soothed to discover that such choices, among other pains and horrors, are the everyday lot

* See footnote page xiii.

of even the most experienced translators: sacrifice is the order of the day. Words and interpretations lie bleeding on the altars of the many Gods, of Euphony, Emphasis, Intention, Accuracy, Alliteration, Ambiguity, Wit. But to me, who when I am waiting for the phone to ring, feel in my secret heart that I should be 'writing', translation is a curious and pleasing evasion. It doesn't engender the often bleak stretches or require the quality of time and concentration that writing from scratch does – someone else has already been through all that for you. It doesn't require you to sit in front of a lonely blank sheet – beside the sheet you have a text and a specific job to do, you have dictionaries and reference books and sometimes even an author to help. The work may be maddening and difficult but it is to some degree measurable. It exposes your ignorance rather more than your soul. There is progress and the occasional feeling of inspiration as well as difficulty. It is easier to keep going. And even the things you postpone can be listed.

It was so nice, too, to have some reply when people asked what I was doing. I could tell that it sounded impressive to be 'translating some monologues' – even grand, efficient, motivated, really on the ball. In this way I came to mention them chatting to the director Stuart Burge, whose neighbour I had become. He said he'd be interested to see them. Stuart's eminence and great experience placed him beyond my wildest hopes should I get to the stage of performance; but I sent the first drafts to him, pursued him with them by mail to California where he was working for a few months. By this time mentioning had become a habit and I mentioned the pieces to Ian McDiarmid and Jonathan Kent at the Almeida Theatre one day in Autumn. It turned out that they were doing a German season in the Spring, including Wedekind's *Lulu*, and were interested in doing some Sunday shows to expand the theme. Thus it came about that, the following April, I performed four of the pieces on two successive Sunday nights. But before that it had also come about, as these things so often do, that I got a job and so found myself rehearsing full time at the National in Steven Pimlott's production of *The Miser* by Molière, while at the same time trying to adapt, learn and rehearse four monologues, average length twenty-five minutes.

I was thrilled that Stuart agreed to direct *Desdemona* and surprised. (I sometimes wondered whether he was quite surprised too. If there is anything more painful than being the only source of error on stage – going wrong, acting badly, forgetting your lines – it must be sitting there, watching.) There was no point even in starting to learn until he came back from California and we could make a final choice of which ones to do, and read them together to discover where to edit them. So that there was no preliminary work that I could do to make up for the overlapping rehearsals. Yet for some reason it did not occur to me to postpone the performances. Perhaps I knew myself well enough to know the limits of my perseverance.

Once Stuart was back we met, when he was free after my rehearsals, where we could, made our choice of the four pieces that would make up the evening: Katharina Luther, Laura, Christiane von Goethe and Clytaemnestra. I read them out, we established the first cuts, I spent my lunch-breaks and weekends and late nights and early mornings trying to learn lines and praying, once they started fitfully to sink in, that we would not have to make cuts. Until I learned my lines there was only a certain amount that Stuart could do and I did feel sorry for him having to sit and watch me flounder for so much of the time. He was spared a little and I was blessed by my having a friend round the corner, Jill Meller, who not only heard me at odd and inconvenient times, but managed to enjoy it. She had not had much to do with the theatre and even seemed to find my struggles to remember, to make links, and to find the four women in the lines, not tedious but fascinating. Her interest was of a special order, intelligent, sustained and tremendously sustaining. Certainly without Jill I would have been sunk, psychologically as well as practically – she even agreed at the last minute to act as prompter. The dependence of actors on so many other people before they can get to the stage, let alone on it, becomes dramatically apparent in a one-person show. Steven Pimlott absolved me from a Saturday morning rehearsal so that I could have a run-through on the *Lulu* set with our props, including Stuart's huge and weighty family pastry-board – we started with Katharina Luther making bread. During the dress rehearsal on Sunday afternoon I noticed flecks of red paint on the mixing bowl. To my surprise, as I observed with that small portion of my brain which was not engaged in willing me on with the scene, they seemed to increase and drop into the dough, while I steadfastly kneaded them in. It was some time before I realise that I had cut myself on the chipped rim of the bowl, and I was kneading my own blood. There must be a lesson there, surely?

Just writing about this is as good as or worse than going to a Greek play, since it fills me with re-lived terror. Whether or not it purges me I can't be sure. The terror was very great and came in waves. From time to time when I tried to think what could be worse than what I had let myself in for, I reminded myself that the original plan had been to do *three* shows on *three* consecutive Sundays with three *different* pieces in each. *The Miser* saved me from this grisly scheme, whose overweeningness I had been peculiarly slow to spot; but as I struggled to do justice to all concerned, rehearsing and learning day and night in between rehearsing and learning, I felt small gratitude. When the 'half' was called – that moment of truth – I sat in disbelief in the bleak and lonely dressing room, filled with other people's props and costumes and make-up, trying to pull my mind round at least to the first of my women, Katharina, but in fact thinking only that it was all my doing, my fault, my blame. As 'beginner'* was called my improvised wimple, which had been sitting beautifully, suddenly twisted and began to undo itself . . .

It went well in the end, clearly a lot better than I thought while I was doing it. I could only feel dazed amazement that I had got through. On both evenings. Both were entirely different. It took me a long time and a lot of people before I began to believe that the audience had liked it. Even my big brother had liked it. It was especially pleasing that each of the four incarnations had her particular fans. Once it was all over and the deed done I could turn back to full-time wrestling with Molière and the character of Frosine. I probably would think twice now before taking so much on again. But exhausting as it was, the pressure of working on both shows certainly seemed to increase my concentration – 'more is more'? (Or perhaps it was just another case of Johnsonian focusing of the mind.) And,

* A 'series of calls' are given over the tannoy before any theatre performance, so that actors and technicians know how much time they have before the show starts. Each call is five minutes more than the 'real' time, so those who begin the performance are in place well before the start. The 'half' is called at thirty-five minutes, 'the quarter' at twenty, the 'five' at ten, and finally 'beginners' at five.

because I have that sort of mind, I couldn't help wondering how would I have felt if it had been a total disaster?

Even from a wreck I would have made salvage, I think: the pleasure of rediscovering German and spending some time with (being helped by) Eva Paneth; trying my hand at translation; working at the Almeida; working with Stuart. And, earlier on, on another visit to Germany, I had an opportunity to meet Christine Brückner, who was as friendly and generous as her writing. I hope in these translations I have managed to convey some of the flavour and freshness of her work. What more can I say?

Yours,
Eleanor Bron

# You're wrong,

# Lysistrata!

Megara, the courtesan,

addresses Lysistrata and the

women of Athens

# Megara

*Aristophanes, the Athenian comic dramatist, wrote a group of anti-war plays during the Peloponnesian War between Athens and Sparta (431–404 BC). In* Lysistrata *written in 411 BC, the women of Athens, led by Lysistrata, seize the Acropolis and the Treasury of Athens and she urges them further to refuse to sleep with the men until they have made peace with Sparta. No character called Megara appears in the play, but it may be worth noting that Megara was one of the three Furies, the Erinyes. A temple was dedicated to them in Athens, where they were renamed and honoured as the Eumenides – the Benevolent Ones – because they had shown clemency to Orestes after he had murdered his mother, Clytaemnestra.*

# You're wrong,
# Lysistrata!

Megara, the courtesan, addresses Lysistrata
and the women of Athens

Listen to *me*, Lysistrata. Listen well. And the rest of you, too.
I have more experience of men than you. You only know your
own husband, Lysistrata, and you think the way he is is the
way they all are. I know a great many. You are asking of the
women of Athens that they forswear the conjugal couch until
such time as the men have concluded the peace. Well, that's
a laugh! Abstinence is the very tinder of aggression! And apart
from that, the war's already been going on for two decades; most
of the women of Athens are widows – who are they supposed
to refuse themselves to? They're looking for someone they can
*give* themselves to!

Just you listen, all of you, to what a courtesan of no mean
experience has to tell you. Why do you always only believe
what men say? You want to *do* something, Lysistrata – that's
good. It's just that what you're demanding is wrong. 'Make them

3

crazy, drive them wild!' Well, I'm with you there, as far as that goes. *But* – you don't really understand what it is that makes them tick. One 'no' too many and they're already turning their lust for women into the lust for battle; swapping the love-nest for the battlefield; all they want to do in either place is to conquer. With your 'no' you are strengthening their thirst for battle, not weakening it. When they've had what they want and are satisfied, then they ask nothing more than to sleep. Am I right, Myrrhina? You really love your husband, I know, and he loves you – from what one hears, the two of you carry on something chronic, like a proper pair of turtle doves. When you turn them down, they go off and find a tart and shell out good money for something that costs nothing at home, and that you could do with yourselves. The girls can't afford abstinence, and courtesans are too canny.

Lysistrata – you want to refuse your husband? Well . . . he hasn't exactly been expecting a great deal from you in that area for a long time, has he? It's no use you stopping your ears!

You are all just as much to blame for the war! You let it happen! Doing nothing is also doing something. What are you saying, Lysistrata: 'We're only women'? Only? I refuse to be a party to that! You haven't thought things through, Lysistrata! Men will promise anything as long as you show willing. Once they are satisfied, their passion for war quickly reasserts itself. Desire is a renewable commodity.

How can you possibly maintain that the individual counts for nothing, Lysistrata? You talk like the men! They say that the individual is nothing, a zero. But a lot of zeros only add up to a lot of zeros – not to one great, united whole. On the battlefield, numbers are important; but women are only effective when they are alone with one man. Isn't that so? I converse quite a lot with philosophers. They seek out conversation with me, because at home they have to put up with a Xanthippe! You complain that your men weigh you down with their endless demands – that's their version. Apparently the more usual pleasures aren't satisfying enough for them. Well, each of you can get specific details from me, individually; I don't want to discuss it in public. But if you would like to know what it is I talk about with the men: they ask me where do the clouds come from, and what atoms are. We talk about things that we don't understand; we exchange uncertainties. One thing I will say to you: no man ever found himself dreaming about tyranny or revolt against the state after sleeping with a courtesan. 'Battle' and 'War' are words which may not be used in our presence with impunity. Far from it – with us the joking and tippling goes on until cock-crow; then they sleep peacefully, and go on resting their weary loins far into the day.

Wherever I look I see widows and widows-in-waiting. Why don't you learn a thing or two from the courtesans? You want to have heroes for husbands! You require medals! You want to boast about their great deeds! Get this into your heads once and for all: a live husband without medals is better than a dead conqueror stretched out on his shield. What do you keep on polishing their spears for, until they glitter? Hide your heroes' weapons from them; put your own in their place!

Lay your youngest child at your breast, and spray a bit of milk out for him too – he's like a child himself, after all, who needs a bit of a cuddle. Kylla will give you some instruction on how to make yourselves beautiful, if you aren't any more – or never were. Camomile has a nice clean smell, Euratea, but it's not seductive. If you're on the skinny side, pad yourselves out a bit! You're not going to get very far just on your beautiful souls. Beauty only comes into her own when she joins forces with a bit of brains. Why on earth do you despise the courtesan's arts? Learn from us! Has a bumblebee got tangled up in your clothing? Whereabouts? You yourselves know best: you know the place that the bumblebee likes to seek out . . . No. Ampelis, it's no good blushing *now* – save your rosy cheeks up for the evening. You've got a nice, taut belly – I can see that a mile off; this evening just make sure it gets seen close to! And you Phryne, as far as I can tell from here, you've got a beautiful little bottom – flaunt it! And what have you got against make-up? You all run around with faces like beetroots. I'm talking about you Myrrha, most of all! Put some powder on, all of you! And the pale ones should paint cheeks on themselves like rosy-red apples. You let all your make-up lie about gathering dust just because there's a war on. A woman who looks the worse for wear is all the more easy to leave behind with a light heart!

Tomorrow morning at the first cock-crow the men will hurry down to the ships. The war is going on. Stop them! The man who leaves his house tomorrow morning has a bad wife, or a stupid one, who doesn't know how to cure his penchant for fighting, how to wear his limbs to a frazzle. Tomorrow morning the streets of Athens are to be bathed in calm. No clattering of weapons first thing after cock-crow. And anyone who doesn't love her own husband – yes, it is possible! – well then, let her love her brother-in-law, or her neighbour. I implore you, not to be petty at this moment in time! Make some sacrifices, if that's what you want to call them – after all you do adore sacrificing yourselves. Unite! Where there's no other remedy, fight over the men, make them lust after you. Tonight Athens is to be one big joyous knocking-shop. Put a stick of incense in the fire, early on: let the smell of cooking waft through the doors, and when he asks what all the haute cuisine's in aid of, say: it's for tomorrow, when we women of Athens are sitting together grieving over our menfolk . . . Slaughter your best fowl and say that you want to sacrifice it next day to the Goddess: consent to roast it for him *today*, only after he has begged you on his bended knees. Get hold of some oil of myrrh, anoint your hair. And, just for once, show a little solidarity: give some to your friend! Help each other with your beautifications! Scrutinise each other carefully but lovingly! Pray to Aphrodite, but whatever you can do for yourselves – do it!

Give your husbands quails' eggs! If you can't rustle any up, at least be sure to get some celery, and cut the green sticks into pieces; you yourselves will have to be the best judges of how long they should be . . . ! Grate the white root finely. Say that you feel hot sitting by the fireside; uncover your shoulders, lift up your petticoat, pull down your dress, let's see those breasts! And don't – please – for the love of Heaven – turn around now and give me all this stuff about Honour and Virtue! Athens is at stake. War demands sacrifices – so does Peace.

'Come here, my little chicken', or my lion, or my bull – whatever your particular mating call is these days – whatever goes to his head, and uplifts any other part of him . . . But hesitate a little; hold him off a while; remember Lysistrata's words. Stick some lemon blossom in your hair, prepare a banquet for him, and sigh – quite involuntarily – that perhaps it may be the last one he'll have, ever. Wear your hair loose, Ampelis – you have such beautiful hair – but turn away from him; and then he will take hold of those lovely locks and

7

draw you towards him and sigh; and then *you* sigh too –
that in future all you will have to look forward to is the
donkey.

Thula! They say that you know a magic potion. Magick
them all! Let them all stagger through the streets, lubricious
and lascivious as Pan himself. Make them jealous! Disguise
your handwriting and write MELISSA LOVES CHAIREAS!
on the walls of your house. The neighbours will read it,
and so will Chaireas, and everyone will believe what it
says. Jealousy sets Love on fire. Melissa? Why are you
avoiding my eye? Have I hit the nail on the head? All
the better! Reduce the town to riot and disorder. What
man can abandon Athens when everything's at sixes and
sevens!

In case he should reach for the water jug, to mix his wine,
fill both jugs with wine. And if there's absolutely nothing
for it, and he demands his shield and his spear – put
some valerian in the last goblet, and he'll sleep like a
baby. Promise that you'll wake him up at the very first
cock-crow. Then when he wakes up in the middle of the
morning, make as if you had overslept, and say that the
other warriors have been aboard the ships long since, but
if he wants to run down quickly through the streets now, all
on his ownsome, he might just catch a glimpse of them in the
distance.

Is your husband's old mother still living in your house?
Or his agèd father, you say? In that case, leave your houses
and go to Lykabettos, there where the spring gushes out
from under the three eucalyptus trees. You know the place
– it's really idyllic. The ground is a soft bed of clover and
lotus, the last of the hyacinths are still scenting the air.

The hedge sparrows sing until late in the evening, and they have scarcely stopped singing, when the owl starts to call . . . Dress yourselves up! But anything that's prettier left uncovered – uncover it. Let your maids fill your baskets full of the choicest foodstuffs (don't forget to decorate them with hibiscus blossom), and put the heavy wine from Samos out to cool in plenty of time, should you still have any wine in your cellars. Then invite your husbands – who will have been watching all your carryings-on full of misgivings–: 'You are welcome to come too, Laches! Pamphilos, come with us! Let us commemorate the last of this little fragment of peace.' The evening light will burnish your bodies like the pillars of the Acropolis at twilight. The goblets will gleam, so that you can see your own reflection in them. Make ready some beds out of myrtle branches; but beforehand – feast! drink! As soon as night falls and the moon climbs up the sky, the youngest women and the most beautiful will bathe themselves in the waters of the spring. There's a light wind blowing, like a zephyr – that will die down later on; it will be a mild night. Nevertheless: take a couple of blankets with you, otherwise the cool of the early morning might sober your slumberers up. And you, Lysis, you will sing! Sing your songs, the ones you only usually sing at the fountain.

Do you feel desire rising in your thighs? That's good. That's what I wanted. Desire is a fever that is catching. An epidemic will spread throughout the length and breadth of Athens. We have to sap the men's strength, not goad them on. The Goddess Athene doesn't have to be the only one who's striving for peace. Help her along! Don't always keep depending only on the Gods.

That is my plan for today. But what about tomorrow? With all our wiles we can't prevent that warmongering spirit from building up again in our menfolk. They will go to the market square and talk and talk and go on talking until they make their own words come true and then they are obliged to reach for their weapons.

So now, Lysistrata, pay attention! I have some plans as to how things should proceed. If they want to wage their war, we must go on strike. *Except* in bed – as I have already said. What have you been doing up to now? You polish up their helmets till they shine, scratch the rust off their shields; and when the bold warrior sets out, you wave goodbye and have a little cry; and then you set to work: keep the house in order, bring up the children, till the fields, press the grapes; and when the battle has been waged, you weave garlands for the living and wreaths for the dead. You revere the heroes and make war as pleasant for them as it is possible to do. But now things are going to change. Let your fields lie untilled. The birds can help themselves to the ripe grapes. Do as much as will keep you and your children from starving, but don't for goodness' sake wear yourselves to the bone. In the end all the honour goes to him, anyway, not to you. And it's not any different for the Spartan women, either. We must join forces with the wives of the enemy. We're supposed to play the man's role in wartime and the woman's role in peacetime. Why should that be? Did you ever see men take up women's jobs? Suckling the children, plying the distaff, baking the bread? You do the men's work on top of that. You gather the harvest before the autumn rains set in; you take the lame horse to the smith and the smith's wife hammers him out new shoes. You mend the roof and have no time to make yourselves beautiful or adorn yourselves. Who for?

So when they come back from the battle – if they do come back! – they find you've become physical wrecks. Full of pride, you display your pitchers of seedcorn, and you actually get ticked off because they are not full enough. The very next day they push you aside – and you make way for them!

In future, when they want to celebrate their victories, say: the pitchers are empty; you have only got a couple of onions in the house, a handful of dry beans from last summer, which you would gladly soften in a little water and cook for him, if the last pot hadn't been broken yesterday and there were no new pots to be had at the potter's; you don't know the first thing about catching fish, so – alas! – you can't steam him a little fish with sage. The oil jar has been empty for ages, the winepress is not working any more – all rusted up; both the donkeys have run away – the rope rotted. (You can hide the donkeys somewhere.)

And, please, in future, just don't be so petty! If your neighbour, who is too old for the war, gives you the glad eye – well! His arms may not be up to wielding a sword any more, but then his strength will go into another of his members. And don't you despise young boys either! Introduce them, with a gentle hand, to real life – I'll say no more. Enjoy each other! Why should we live in abstinence? Just because the men are away? Faithfulness is alright as long as you are together. We'll soon spoil the fun of their wars, we women of Athens and Arcadia, of Boeotia and of Sparta. Take a look at the Erechtheum! Does anything strike you? The heavy burden of that roof is borne not, as with other temples, by pillars, but by women! Do you see what I'm saying? They build on our strength!

11

Hear me out! Stay sat, Corinna! I haven't finished yet! It isn't only the men who think about Athens, we do too; it's our town, too, and we want to live in it – with the men. A man who loves his life doesn't gamble with it all that willingly; instead he carves a pony for his little son, fixes up a swing in the fig tree . . . I know your husbands – most of them at least. They are like children. They don't have enough to do, they have to be kept busy. The man who tills his own fields won't be so keen to turn them into battlegrounds; and it's not any different in Attica to how it is in Sparta. It's the man who is at a loose end who gets into fights. You must know that from your children.

Praise your neighbour's house: give a hint that it's more spacious and cooler than yours – he must be cleverer or more hard-working. And before you know it, he'll be reaching for the shovel. His brother's water supply is better. That must be because he's had his well dug deeper. In summer, because your well has dried up, you have to lug the pitchers all the way to your brother-in-law's – not that you mind in the least . . . (with a meaning look!) Spur his efforts on, mention Athens, always have the good of the city in view, point out the importance of what he is doing – he needs to be acknowledged. And make his evening – and yours – a real delight: light torches, let your little boy play naked in the courtyard; compare him, in all innocence, with his father.

Ampelis! Musarion! Stay here! Are you off home to patch up your widow's weeds? Well, yes – you'll surely be needing them soon. Why not put your tragic faces on this very minute, and practise wailing!

The men are not to hand out good gold for armaments and weapons. We protest! We want a say in how our taxes are to be spent. Why weapons? Why not storage jars, hair clasps, sandals? They are out to defend every last paving stone of Athens, every inch of Attica. They will prolong this war until we are all starving, until we are forced to eat our own pet cat ourselves, before our neighbours lay hold of it. And consider one thing: it is mothers who have brought these men up to be like this! If no one had said to them: 'You are a man, be brave! Don't cry!', they would be just as fearful as we are. You should all let your sons play with the spinning wheel and when you comfort them say: 'Just have a good cry! Men are allowed to cry too! People who can cry know how to laugh as well.' Male fortitude gives me the pip! Why don't we go with them to the market square? When they vote for going on with this war we will vote against. Our voices are lighter and more penetrating. When they cry 'War!', we will cry 'Peace!'

Teach them to savour *life*. Fighting is not the pinnacle of achievement. Death on the battlefield is not the most beautiful. The gold that their campaigns cost should be used to benefit our cities. We know only too well how meagre are the spoils of war. They think that we can't add up, that we don't know what a day of peace yields, compared to the cost of one day of war. Why do you all make out that you are stupid? Why don't you do the sum for them?

Lysis, vault up on to the wall and sing them one of your satirical songs – but don't push it! They are so easily hurt. We are here to love and not to hate. The Gods have allotted us such a little span. Our youth is so brief! Our beauty leaves us so soon! We must make use of the years we have.

13

Why are you all running away? Stay, please; at least until I have finished. Thula! Myrrhina! We shall throw ourselves on their shields when they reach for them. And if even that is no use, then you say: 'I am going with you! I will not abandon you and I will be at your side, through thick and thin. I would rather be dead than live without you.' The old people, too; agèd father, blind mother, children, nobody stays behind! Make it clear that you don't want to outlive them. You want to live in peace or not at all. Say: 'Give me your spare spear, I can throw it like Athene! I have practised on the fields that were lying fallow. You, Lysistrata, you throw far better than your husband. Doesn't the thought of battle tempt you? War is an adventure! Enjoy yourselves. If your dresses are too confining, bare your breast; anoint your limbs with oil, like the men; shout out that you are going to hurl yourselves upon the Spartans!

And now for the last part of my plan, Lysistrata! What is so different about the men of Sparta? They say that their ears stand out like handles on a jug. Good. Grab them by their handles! They are supposed to be strong – well that suits you all right doesn't it? The beauty of the Attic women will enchant the Spartans. At the right moment – the *last* moment – we exchange men's weapons for women's. We will weaken the Spartans' powers. It must all take place at night-time. We creep into their camp, barefoot, unarmed. And then, when our own men realise where we are, they take care of the rest!

Myrrhina – little dove! Now you're running off again, too! So now it's just us, Lysistrata. They won't follow your plan. Nor mine. It will all go on in the old way, just as it always has. . . .

# *Are you sure,*

# *Martinus?*

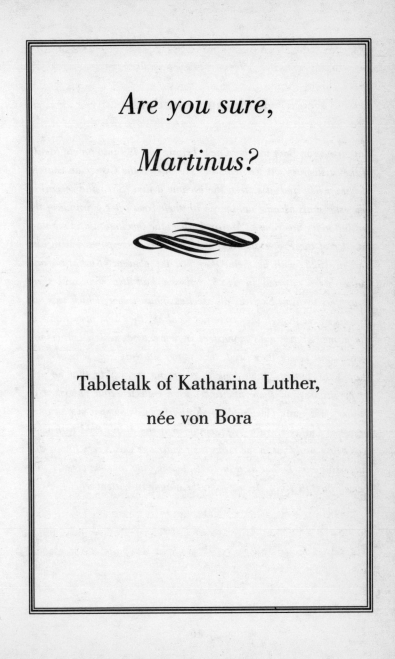

## Tabletalk of Katharina Luther,
### née von Bora

# Katharina von Bora

*Katharina von Bora was born near Leipzig in 1499 into an old family of the aristocracy. At ten years old she entered the Cistercian convent of Nimpschen and at sixteen she became a nun. She, and several of her sister nuns became unhappy with their vows after learning of the revolutionary doctrines of Martin Luther, the theologian and scholar, founder of the Protestant Reformation. They corresponded with him and in 1523, with his help, they fled the convent. Katharina and Luther were married in 1525 and she had two sons and three daughters by him. She was an excellent housekeeper, which was just as well since, though they were not wealthy, they kept open house at the former Augustinian monastery in Wittenberg, which Luther now owned and where they lived. The many students and scholars who shared the Luthers' table took to recording everything that he said at mealtimes and these utterances were collected and published as Luther's* Tabletalk *(Tischreden). Katharina was outspoken and often provoked Luther's wrath by chipping in if she didn't hold with what was being said, but in the main their marriage was a very happy and successful one. Luther died in 1546, leaving her in some poverty. She herself died in 1552, fleeing from the plague in Wittenberg.*

# Are you sure,
# Martinus?

Tabletalk of Katharina Luther,

née von Bora

Today, at table, Martinus, you said that if ever you had the chance to do your courting over again, you would carve yourself a woman out of stone; you despair of ever finding an obedient woman any other way.

I thought I left all those old vows behind me, when I left the convent. Poverty, Obedience, Chastity – each one in turn. Well – poverty is certainly taken care of! Count how many heads at your table. Every time we sit down I count the number of mouths, all wanting to be fed. Eleven orphans of our kinsfolk, plus our own five, makes sixteen children; three widows; plus the scholars who cling on to survival at our expense, and the servants on top of that – that guarantees that poverty is daily perpetuated.

You call me Domina, as if I ruled over this house like a Mother Superior. Twenty good little nuns, who pray a good deal and eat very little, would be a mere bagatelle! Instead of that here I am looking after forty or fifty folk, as if we were running an inn in Wittenberg, in the Augustan cloister – 'At the sign of the Blessed Lamb'. A good, cheap place to stay, not to mention the honour.

So – we come to Obedience. Are you my Abbot? Or my confessor? Or are you my husband? Why do you keep on saying: 'Let the woman show obedience to her spouse'? A good old rage really sets you up, doesn't it? Well, me too! 'Be ye angry and sin not. Let not the sun go down upon your wrath!' That's what it says in Ephesians Four. The sun's going down in a few minutes from now, Martinus. Every morning, when I say my Our Father, I have to crave an extra boon: I pray, give me this day my daily portion of good will. But it never does last until the evening.

Why shouldn't the husband have to obey the wife too? In the Epistle to the Ephesians doesn't it also say we are all members one of another? I know it's different in your translation. Really, when we see to the children's wants, aren't we obeying them? Don't you think really it's the children who have brought me up? When they demanded the breast I gave it to them, didn't I? When they cried, I cradled them and rocked them in my arms. I was obeying them. That's how we are members one of another. In the beginning, I'm the one who's chasing about after the chickens but in the end, when the bird is roasted and sits there on the table, it's she that's doing our bidding and filling our bellies.

If it takes patience for you to live with me, I need patience to live with you, too. I live with 'Luther, the Preacher'; and how I wish it wasn't only wise old Solomon's sayings that were handed down to us, but a couple of observations from his wife as well, to give me a few pointers.

18

And now I come to the vow of chastity. You haven't stopped being a monk and I haven't stopped being a nun. We have the same background, Martin. Every time we lie together you say: 'And they shall be one flesh.' But you have never believed it; and no more have I. We have never had much pleasure from it, and if either of us ever was aroused we only felt ashamed, like Adam and Eve when they were cast out of Paradise.

I know as well as you do that another of the things it says in Ephesians is: 'Let every one of you in particular so love his wife even as himself, and let the wife see that she fear her husband.' But I don't want to fear my own husband; and I won't – even if he is the famous Martin Luther. It's hard enough to love you all the time, and for you too it's hard enough to love me and put up with me; don't ask for obedience into the bargain! I go about my business as best I can, and you carry out your work, and then on top of that we have some work in common and that is God's work, I obey Him and I fear Him. If, one day, God is going to look mercifully upon me, then you can jolly well do the same right now!

There – that's out . . . Now I feel better. I'll fetch us a jug of beer and we'll take it to the bedroom to drink, and no one is going to be writing down what we say to each other before we drop off to sleep. And tomorrow morning, God willing, you'll call me your darling Morning Star again, and you won't be amazed and ashamed to find two dark pigtails beside you on the pillow.

Are you sure, Martinus? How can it be that we may not find peace while we are still alive, but only once we are in the grave? And can you find peace – the way you find mushrooms in the forest and wild berries, or a lost shoe? Peace is something that

you have to make, the way you and I do, every evening. Make
it and keep it. You have to fight for peace and struggle for it.
Peace has to be painstakingly forged. If there is peace in every
house there is peace throughout the land.

But the trouble is, nothing is for ever. Every morning we
start out afresh with our good resolutions and sure enough
they don't last until suppertime. So – now that you have said
grace, Martinus, I ask leave to speak. Before our meal your
prayer was:

'Come take, dear Lord, with us Your place,
And share this food, Your gift of grace.'

Today, sitting at the end of the table, we have an Unbeliever,
who will go forth and tell everyone throughout the length and
breadth of the land how things are done in Dr Luther's house in
Wittenberg. He has taken down zealously every word that all
of you have been saying. You ought to have adapted grace this
time and asked: '. . . share this man, your gift of grace.' And if
I had said grace after supper, I should not only have thanked
God, I should have thanked Hannes, who chopped the wood
so that we could light the fire, and little Mary, who helped me
to shred the cabbage, and Farmer Pflock, who killed a pig and
brought us a pail of sausage broth, and perhaps you could even
for once have thanked your Katharina for seeing to it that today,
just as on every other day, everyone had enough to eat.

What was it you were proclaiming just now, not for the first
time, in the presence of forty eager pairs of flapping ears? That I
have a pious husband? I am an Empress and should give thanks
to God? And I say: you, Martinus, have a pious wife, you are an
Emperor – thank God for it! And now all your learned disciples
are laughing, but the only thing they are noting down, is that I

have an Emperor for a husband. And that's the way it goes at Luther's house.

I didn't have any choice, Martinus. You were the first, and in the end you have turned out quite simply to be the best. A runaway nun, twenty-four years old already, no beauty, and poor with it. My one little smidgeon of a marriage portion went to the nunnery; and in those days I wasn't even halfway decent as a housekeeper yet, either. You did me a good turn. But haven't I done you quite a few good turns too – over the years? You used to sleep on a straw pallet that was only ever given a shake-out about once a year. And you said that you used to be crawling with desires like fleas and lice; and for quite a few years now, you've been living in what can only be described as a well-ordered domesticity. I try to lead a life that will find favour in God's sight; but that sometimes seems to me to be a lot easier than leading a life that will find favour in yours. I am a canny Saxon woman – you knew that! You won't often find me at a loss for words; but aren't I always the soul of discretion as far as you're concerned? Of what passes in our bedchamber, to the outside world – never a hint. I have learned something, in all these years of marriage: whenever you are feeling downhearted, that's when I recognise your greatness; but when you start assuming the mantle of a superman, then it's only too easy to cut you back down to size. I don't have the measure of all things within me, but the measure of Martin Luther, I do have.

And now will you just take a look at how Cranach has painted us! He has painted you taller and more powerful than you are, and he has made me scraggier. In years to come people will say: 'Look – there you go again: proof that in any marriage only one partner can prosper; and with the Luthers in Wittenberg he was the one to grow sleek and stout, whereas she's worn out before her time.' My eyes don't slant as much as that, and my cheekbones aren't that high; and my hair is not as black as he has painted it any more. Now, instead of people forming their own picture of us, they see us through this man Cranach's eyes.

You are out of sorts, Martinus. And it's not even a week ago that you were declaring to all of us at table that according to the law of Moses, anyone who is miserable should not be admitted to the altar or to the sacrifice. I have prepared a tea for you that's very good for the miseries. *Achillea millefolium*, the common yarrow – it grows on the old grave behind the wall. I have let it seethe in red wine. Drink it up now while it's still hot, so that you don't infect us all with your gloom. Gloom is the worst malady of all and I will not tolerate it under our roof. And there are you, writing your hymns: 'Rejoice, rejoice all you good Christian souls and let us all skip joyfully!'

Drink up! Rejoice! Jump for joy! You're getting fat, you stuff yourself too much. You lay all your ills at the Devil's door, but the fact is you simply ate too much of the cabbage at lunch today.

Do I have to remind you of your own sermon? Wasn't it just a little while ago that you recounted one of your beautiful parables, where a wise old man says to a young man: 'You cannot keep the birds from flying about back and forth up in the air above you, but from nesting in your hair! You can certainly prevent them doing that!'

I cannot stand having a husband who writes one thing and lives another. It's laughter that drives the Devil out of the house. It's Joy and Trust that are his adversaries. So drink up, Martinus! and don't quarrel with your God any longer. He's used to people quarrelling with Him; just as long as he doesn't pick a quarrel with you – that's the main thing!

Do you ever have any idea what it is you are eating, Martinus? I put a fine dish of goose giblets in front of you, and even as you sit there tucking in, you're saying things like: 'You can throw a donkey rosemary for fodder and he'll think he's eating hay!' And what do you think you're eating – groats?

And then on top of that, you maintain that it's always the wicked who enjoy the best of Our Lord's gifts: the tyrants have the power, and the peasants have the cheese and eggs, butter, corn, barley and a lot more besides – only the Christians are left to languish in the tower, and there, neither sun nor moon ever shine upon them. Look out of the window! Isn't that the sun shining on us? Haven't we got our barley on our plates? Haven't you got more than you could wish for? Don't you have things that other people lack? And your Belief to comfort you into the bargain?

Stop complaining, Martinus. Don't make people more dissatisfied than they already are. Do you envy the Powers-that-be their power? Don't you have more power than you ever wanted? Don't people act just as if they were duty-bound to carry out the commandments of Dr Martin Luther of Wittenberg? Little children groaning out loud, because they have to learn your catechism by heart? You are a part of the Powers-that-be yourself, and when people in church pray for their rulers – because of their high position, which lays greater obligations upon them than on their subordinates, who only have to do what they are told – then it may be that one or other of them will include you in his prayers; and nothing surely could be better than that: having somebody praying for you!

Ah, Doctorus, you really are such a wise man! You say that by nature human beings act out of hindsight, rather than from forethought. All our knowledge comes from the pain of past experience, and we have had to pay dearly for our lessons. You said human beings but you meant men. Women are different. They look forwards, not backwards so much. God put our eyes up at the front, so that we could look ahead, not behind. What makes you wiser is your misfortunes – me, my foresight. Oh, we're both such clever people!

That was the dearest and the best thing you ever said about our marriage: that it was chaste, and superior to any celibacy. We have known both: what it is to lie in a cell all alone with your desires; and what it is to lie side by side as desires transform themselves into love. (But what you were saying over soup on the other hand, no that was not right: an adulteress brings a strange heir into the house. You see the thing from a purely legal standpoint. A bastard is also one of God's children and ought not to be punished for the sin that his mother has committed.) People take their lead from what you say; and they take their lead from the way we live. And if what comes out of your mouth tomorrow is what I've been saying to you today, then I shouldn't let it upset me. If we are one flesh we ought to be one spirit too.

I'm taking you at your word, Martinus! You have just quoted a passage from Jesus Sirach: 'He who disdains the head of the chicken shall receive no other share.' Here you have got the head – now don't you disdain it! Today the gentlemen students are getting the white meat of the breast, because they have been so diligently writing down all the things the renowned Dr Luther has been saying at table – not for the first time. For example, you said that God created mankind to live in society and not in solitude; that was the reason for there being males and females. But in that case Martinus and Katharina Luther would be sitting alone at your table. And how many are there today? I count thirty-seven.

At 'my' table, you said, but the truth is, isn't it, that it's at our table that we sit down together to eat. You also said 'My little boy'; but isn't he my son too? Oughtn't you to have said 'our' son? And just before, you said again 'my' God; you have a personal God, that's perfectly reasonable; but here, at this table, it's the God of all of us, and the Jesus Christ of all of us, whom we invite to take a place at our table. It's not even as if you didn't ever sometimes say 'we'. Katy, we really must brew some more beer! Katy, we must mend the roof! 'We must' – that means: you do it, Katharina, you see to it; Katharina, brew the beer, get the roof mended. And now you're laughing, Martinus, and you put your hand on my hand and both our hands are lying on our table!

Have you got all that down, all you scholars? Or can you only do your special shorthand in Latin? And of course you can't write Saxon as fast as I can speak it. So no one will ever hear the whole story of possessive pronouns in Dr Martin Luther's house? Now you're busy writing your fingers to the bone, and writing down word for word what the Great Reformer says at table. Next thing, you'll be creeping along right into our bedchamber as well, and out of sheer good nature he'll say: 'Let's squeeze up a little closer, Katharina, then there'll be room for everyone on our couch.'

Of course he talks to me before he goes to sleep. And when he's dreaming he even talks to the Devil. God he talks to in the daytime. And when he has bad dreams and groans out, so loud that the rafters shake, then I grab him by the shoulders and shake him, and stand by him while he battles through. And when we wake up, we talk to each other then, as well.

What's this? Aren't you noting down what Katharina von Bora says? For some years she was a Bride of Christ and she felt like one of the wise virgins who awaits the bridegroom; and today she would certainly be an Abbess with the Cistercian Sisters.

Now you're staring at me! If you're not writing, then eat! Help yourselves! Eat up! Fill your bellies yet again. Today the last bird is on the table . . . The tubs of smoked meat are empty. It's very nicely planned, that the Lenten fast comes early in the year, when nothing in the garden is growing. When all the sausages have been eaten up. In the summer and autumn, when everything gets ripe and is harvested, none of you would be able to keep your fast. It's good to fast at an empty table. And at Easter the hens start to lay all over again, the cabbage sprouts afresh, the little chicks are born. Until then – no beer! From tomorrow we drink herb tea; that will last until Easter; and purify you body and soul; and keep you sober.

With your left hand you eat what the maids and I have cooked, and with the right you copy down any wise sayings that Dr Luther utters; and then you run to the publishers and to the printers and turn it all into gold, everything that pours out of him, and he himself doesn't take so much as a farthing's fee for all his books and his writing. Isn't it right, then, and very reasonable, that you should pay a little something towards your board, since you are feeding yourselves twice over at our table, with Luther's artistry in theology and mine in the kitchen?

Why don't you eat, Martinus? Why don't you ever leave off talking? The honoured students and scholars don't so much as see what I fetch to the table, let alone taste it. They hang on your every word.

Take a good look at him, all of you, the great Reformer! Now he's holding his hand in front of his face and spreading his fingers out. That's his way of telling me that if you want be a ruler you have to know how to look through your fingers; if you can't do that you don't know how to rule. That's supposed to mean, don't be too hard on them, Katharina. But now I just have to get it out of my system. The citizens of Wittenberg want the prestige and the honour of being known as Luther's town, but they don't want to pay for the privilege. And one day, we're going to have to pawn the last of the silver goblets along with the rest. Nobody gets fat on fame. Do you imagine I never see what it is you're so busy writing? You have informed the world that Katharina Luther is 'the Regent in Heaven and on Earth'. And if ever Dr Luther and his wife were not in accord, then everybody was kept abreast of that, too. But in our own bedstead, there we are as one. As God is our witness. And now, Martinus, say grace, so that I can leave the table.

Martinus, just look at these incredulous faces! For the fifth time just now you told them gold is a barren affair. Why don't you take a handful of coins and go into the garden and stick them all in the soil? Then they'll see what comes up and what doesn't.

They are just like the children! No sooner have you translated the psalms for them, than they want Jesus Sirach translated. A new sermon every four weeks.

Martinus! They are going to go away just now and sell all the things you just said, in a fit of bad temper: that verily we are poor folk, and so the best thing would be for us all to die soon and be buried. You forgot to mention the Resurrection!

27

And if, today, you don't believe in the Resurrection, surely you must at least have believed in the Last Judgement and had fear of that! But perhaps it's good that they should hear these things – even the great Reformer has his troubles and doubts and doesn't shy away from speaking about them. Believing is a difficult business, that's what you really think, and you let them see it; and I of course am the fainthearted one, who thinks that when Luther doubts, God's work comes to grief.

What are you complaining of, Martinus! Even you live from the mistakes that people make. From their sins. When it comes down to it, really, everyone lives from the mistakes of their fellow human beings. We wear our shoes out to give the shoemaker a living, tear our coats for the tailor; feed lawyers on our misdemeanours, doctors on our illnesses, and the gravedigger on our deaths. It's just the same with a parson – he lives off people's sins. Do you really think that any of that will change even if they all learn your little catechism off by heart?

The Wittenbergers address me as Frau Doktor, and not because I am your wife, but because I can heal them. Drink that, Martinus! Horse-dung boiled in wine is good for coughs. I have tried it out on the mare and on the dog. And if you don't want to drink it, then please stop that coughing! Pigshit calms the blood – I smear that on the children's knees when they cut them. So, why not horseshit? I don't know whether red wine is good for gout or not, but it does your temper good and that's good for all of us. And when all the people of Wittenberg run away from the plague, why we'll stay here, if that's what you want. It's fear that makes people ill, I'll give you that; running away is no use.

Today at table you said that our Lord God Himself was the

28

greatest cause of transgression. Why did He make things that way? You spoke about pilfering and adultery and robbery. In the convent, if we left a scrap of lamb on our plate, the Mother Superior would quote from the writings of the Holy Katherine: If it's going to be partridge, let it be partridge; if it's repentance – repentance! So now I think to myself: it has to be a wholehearted sin to yield wholehearted repentance. At least let people enjoy their sinning!

Perhaps that's what God had in mind when He set up the world so full of temptations. I see your eyes following after our maid when she climbs up the stairs in front of you! But you don't take any pleasure in it – you feel ashamed. And shame, Martinus – that's such a little emotion; it doesn't become you. Our Lord causes the pike to grow big and fat, and the good Rhine wine to grow for your delight, so He must have created rounded legs and arms and whatever else of the maid's that is rounded, so that you can enjoy them!

No – please – let me cry, Martinus! Crying is better than quarrelling. God gave us a little child and took him away again. Several times a day you pray: 'Lord, Thy Will be done!' So, now – let it be done! He was really more my child than yours. Not every seedling flourishes, not every cub grows up to be a lion. A child is one of Nature's creatures. One night you'll put your seed inside me again and God will make me fruitful and bless my body. He gave us tears and they melt our quarrels away. I bow down and I raise myself up again. As long as the grief that I bury in the autumn doesn't come up again in the Spring. Really you would have liked to have one of the Schönfeld sisters, but you hesitated for too long and someone else got her. And now it's left up to me to try and please both you and God at the same time.

What happens under this roof carries weight with people. They'll say, the Great Reformer is quarrelling with his God, because God has taken his child back unto himself. But the Truth is, it's Mother Nature that you are quarrelling with. Not everything that she brings forth manages to live. You always want to understand everything, but there are some things we just have to accept – that's one of Nature's lessons. But you never get as far as the trees, you stay sat in your study and hunt in books for things that are there for the reading in the leaves, in the branches.

You ask too many questions, Martinus! Most of your questions have been answered long ago by God in his Creation. I run after the little duckling that's got wet in the rain, I warm it in my apron, I rear it; I hoe between the little cabbage plants; and in the end I put the bird into the pot and I put the cabbage into the pot and I annihilate the thing that I have nurtured. And if I give birth to another child, I will raise it and worry over it and know full well that it has to go, Martinus, sooner or later! We entrust this little creature to the earth and to Heaven, and to Him who has created all things.

Take no thought for the morrow! That's just a lot of male bravado. If you are dying, shouldn't you take some thought for your wife and children? But women and children are not little birds up in the sky. And you ought to be making some provision. According to the law, the widow's portion is a chair and a coat. Let her spin! Let the old woman spin until her fingers bleed! Our house is a permanent building-site and I don't know how I am to pay the workmen and get the servants fed. The Wittenbergers want to bask in Luther's light but they don't want to pay for the privilege. And now you're looking at me again as if to say, 'Katharina, you ought to say your prayers!'

You said, Martinus, that I barge about like a great carthorse instead of reading the Bible. That you would give fifty gilders if I had read it to the end by Easter. I read the Bible for quite long enough in the convent, and now it's high time to put what I've read into action. All right then, you pray! You do my praying – I'll do your working. '*Ora et Labora*', the way we learned, you in your cloister and me in mine. A goose quill doesn't weigh too much! I take up my hoe and my shovel, but I also see to it that you always have a good supply of quills.

In May, when I place a pea in the ground, that's been freshly dug and raked, well that's a prayer; I am entrusting the pea to the earth and to whatever rain God may send us, and to the sun that He causes to shine; so that this pea can produce a meal for all of us. What I'm doing is praying. When I dig, when I sow, when I gather in the harvest. And when I kill a kid, that's praying too. And when I put an egg underneath a broody hen, that's a favour I'm asking. And when I break an egg into the batter, that is saying thank you for all the gifts.

You always talk in parables – why is that? About the good trees that bear good fruit! It's me that takes care that the fruit is good. I have to put lime rings round the trees against pests. I have to make sure that air gets to the roots, I have to prune them. You act as if I'm an out-and-out Martha, and the house lacks a Mary to sit at your feet. But I am Martha and Mary rolled into one! When I stand over the stove stirring my sauces – that's when I have my best thoughts. You don't have to sit in a pew if you want to hear the Lord's word – he speaks to me in the kitchen as well. And I shield Martha from Mary and Mary from Martha. A short time ago you were praying for our sick neighbour, Farmer Pflock. Good! You do that! But what the old man also needs is a good nourishing broth and someone to come and let a little fresh air into his sickroom.

And don't you interfere when I ask God for rain! I can manage soup, but not rain. I pray for the things I can't do myself. Yes! Perhaps tomorrow the world will sink without trace – that's the impression you give. What if you were to go out into the garden and – with your own hand – plant that little apple tree there has been so much talk about? I plant young saplings, apple trees and plum trees and pear trees, whether the world is about to come to an end or not. And you depend upon it. Your Katy will carry on and plant, and God won't let the world come to an end yet, just so that you can keep on sitting at your Luther table writing your parables.

What about this as a parable for you, Martinus? Speech is silver, silence is gold. You are always holding forth to us: women in the congregation should hold their peace. So – would our silence be golden then? Most of the time I do carry my silence about with me like a nugget of gold, and I try to convert it into the small change of daily life.

You say that the spirit has to be nourished daily through study and prayer, because it is ever and always forgetful. It's just the same with bodily nourishment. We eat and excrete. Some of it we use and the rest turns into lard. The word alone is not enough and the deed alone is not enough. That's why men and women live together, so that each one makes the other one whole! And if I didn't open the curtains in the morning and say: 'Martinus, it's Spring!' you would never even notice. Are you actually listening to me at all, Martinus? . . . Martinus? . . . God's blessing on your slumbers!

# Love has found

## a new name

Sick with the plague,
Donna Laura addresses Petrarch,
who has taken flight

# Laura

*Very little is known about Laura, to whom the great Italian poet Francesco Petrarca (Petrarch) addressed his famous love sonnets. It may be that she was not one woman but a composite object of adoration. The most popular theory is that she was the daughter of Audibert de Noves and became the wife of Hugh de Sade, a middle-ranking nobleman of Avignon in Provence. She died of the plague on April 6, 1348.*

*Petrarch (1304–1374) was born in 1304 in Italy but in 1313 his father fled from Florence as a political exile to Avignon, at a time when Provence was under the rule of King Robert of Naples. At this time too Avignon was the residence of the Popes, and the centre of a varied and high-powered society gathered round the high pontiffs of Christendom. Petrarch studied law at Bologna and returned to Avignon in 1326. On 6 April 1327, a Good Friday, he first saw Laura at the Church of Santa Chiara, fell in love with her and began to write the canzoniere:* Rime in vita e morte di Madonna Laura. *In 1330 he entered the service of the powerful Colonna family, in 1337 bought a small property near Vaucluse, which became a centre for his literary work. In 1340 he was invited to Rome to be crowned poet laureate. He is considered to be Italy's greatest lyric poet and through his collecting of books, coins, manuscripts and his devotion to study and self-education he also instigated a revival of learning, especially related to the classics. For this reason he is held to be the founder of humanism and inaugurator of the Renaissance in Italy.*

# Love has found
# a new name

Sick with the plague, Donna Laura
addresses Petrarch, who has taken flight

You have fled, Francesco! You forsook the city when they found
dead rats on the banks of the Rhône. I know you are fearful
– all poets are fearful. You write about death, but it's life you
love. Even the servants have taken flight, except for Milli. She
would have fled, too, but milord de Sade has set a guard before
the house, who lets nobody in and nobody out. She wants to
live. Even *I* want to live. But I am dying, Francesco, I am
dying from the plague, and you are flying from the plague.
Your beautiful image of Donna Laura is quite gone. They will
stick me in a barrel and throw me in the river like the other
dead people. Milli crosses herself when she enters my chamber.
I am tormented by bouts of shivering, and then high fever. Milli
has wrapped blankets round me and pushed hot bricks between
the sheets.

It's just as well you can't see me! I am not like the picture of me that you created any more, Francesco. That first glance in the church of Santa Chiara! It was a Good Friday. In the deathly shadow of the man who had been my lord and master up till then. You faltered under my gaze and had to support yourself against a pillar until I looked away. A smile, when I recognised you a second time, on Easter morning. Our shoulders touched involuntarily. I entered the church through a side door. It was only yesterday. It was twenty years ago! In the beginning, I would have given my life to feel your hand on my cheek just for one moment! To be able to lean my forehead against your forehead. Just thinking of it immediately threw me into a fever. That was a different fever – the fever of youth. Your gaze pierced through my veil, pierced through my eyelids, although I closed them. Petrarch! You punctured my eyelids, night could never fall again!

Immortal Beloved! But I was mortal, Francesco! My love for you was only too mortal. You never asked about my feelings. Oh – if only you had taken me by the hand! One word – I would have followed you. I had courage enough, but it was comeliness you had in mind. I learned to keep my eyes under control and to control my footsteps. I kept my horse on a tight rein. Only once I rashly let it drink at a spring; and then it whinneyed loudly and reared up and ran away with me. The beast had more sense than its mistress. He found his stall, found his manger; a stable boy came and rubbed him down, and Milli came and dragged me away to my chamber, so that no one should see my torn garments. We stitched away at them for a long time. Milli, the procuress! She wanted to steal out by night, to bring you notes. The to-ing and fro-ing of little letters. She wanted to open the gates that led to the courtyard for you – at night-time; wanted to keep watch, the way the maids in other houses did. Or another time, she wanted to lead me, without anyone seeing, to the Colonna's palace, where you lived, where there was supposed to be a side door. I covered my ears, but my hands became like seashells and her words boomed in my ears. I didn't forbid her chattering, the way maids all chatter. Ah, Milli! Nothing – I don't need anything, Milli. Sit by the window!

Your glances kissed my eyes. Hidden behind my veil I saw that your lips formed were forming my name: the L, the A, the U, and R, and A. Then you threw yourself onto your knees – before the portals of the church! In front of milord de Sade. I said quickly, he must have stumbled. Do you know the gentleman? He didn't take you seriously, my husband, otherwise he'd have had to draw his sword. 'A poet!' he said, with a sneer. Later, when he learned your name; when he knew that you lived with the Colonna family, like a son; that you were in and out of the papal court – then it sounded different: A Poet!

I pulled the veil across my face – you seemed to expect it. Another time I pushed it to one side with my hand, as if the wind, that sweeps round the corner of the church, had snatched hold of it. One time I would pretend to be proud, another, soft and gentle; still another, haughty-cruel; and then again, devout and pious. You attributed to me a grace full of modesty. And wildness, as well, and hardness. What did you ever see of my wildness? Did you see the way I dug my spurs into my horse? The way I leapt across the stream with one bound? I was not a heavenly being, I was not an angel. There would be time enough for that later I thought. But how was I to tell you that? You didn't notice any of my signals.

37

I went to that same church always at the same time. And I didn't see you anywhere, Francesco! I turned round and went back a second time, as if I still hadn't prayed enough. I asked my spouse: 'What are they saying about that Signor from Italy – oh, what's his name . . . isn't he called something like Petrurch?' He gave me details. 'He writes letters to kings,' he said, his voice full of respect. 'He stays at royal courts!' I repeated: 'Petrarch writes letters? Is that an occupation for a man?' I made fun of you in front of him, just so that I could speak your name. His parents came from Florence, he went on to tell me; they had to flee. Later he finished his studies in Bologna. He lives in the House of the Colonnas; not like a friend – no – like a brother, like a son. I said: 'Go on!' and 'Really?' I took tiny mouthfuls of food; I asked my husband for another glass of wine, so that he would go on talking about you, although I knew all of it already ages ago, from Milli. Only one sentence I hadn't heard before, which my spouse repeated with respect. 'It is one of Petrarch's,' he said: 'Quite a courageous statement for a poet: "God has commended his little sheep to the Pope, our Holy Father, so that he may feed them, not fleece them."'

I couldn't help laughing! We had roasted lamb on the platter in front of us. I took a piece and crammed it into his mouth, and laughed. I had learned perfectly well by then how you manage a husband, but this time I had done quite the wrong thing. He looked at me gravely, moved my hand to one side, and said: 'I am speaking of a poet!' I am speaking of the Pope, of God! I went on laughing all the same. I was full of myself that day. I wanted to go on talking. The lamb came from the Lubéron; Milli had prepared it in a sauce with fresh mint. He disapproved of my conduct. He emptied his goblet, pushed

38

back his chair and left the room. To come straight back in. Just to say: 'It would be no bad thing if this Petrarch – who appears to hold you in some esteem – could get me admitted into the Colonna household. I smiled, and shrugged my shoulders helplessly. What difference did it make to me, whether milord de Sade went there or not? If we had been rich and had owned an estate beyond the city gates, you would have been in and out of our house, Francesco. We would have sat on the balcony of our palazzo, eating and talking. But what should we have had to say to each other? Talking is a bit different from writing. One is good for now, the other is for always.

Then one day Milli came back from market and pulled a scrap of paper out of her bodice! There was a verse on it that we couldn't read; all I could make out was the name Laura – three times! At the top it said: 'Madonna Laura'. Carlo, who cooks for the Pope and who is an Italian, told her what was on the paper. From now on she found pieces of paper in the marketplace, and then on the bridge. You seemed to scatter them heedlessly, as if no one in the city could read Italian. Before I could find out what was written on the papers, Carlo read it as best he could, and translated it for Milli. She was learning Italian, and so was I – a kind of kitchen-Italian. Why didn't you write in my language – which is so beautiful? You wrote about *amore* and we say *amour*.

'A woman who was lovelier than the sun,
But still more luminous and of the self-same age.'

What did you mean by that? The young sun? Wasn't it already noon?

My monsieur, milord de Sade! Someone let him know what was going on. They spoke of *canzoniere*, not of *chansons*. He read one of your verses out to me.

'Like to no mortal as she treads the earth,
More like to angels; and the words she speaks
Are like no sound from other human lips.'

You had turned Donna Laura into a Saint: Madonna Laura.

'Have you spoken with him?' he asked. I raised my shoulders and said that I hadn't. It was the truth. On not one page you had written was there a single sentence that my confessor might not have read! You loved my Virtue. You wanted to uphold my Virtue. It was the most precious thing about me. In the late afternoon, when it was a bit cooler in the streets and I would go for my little promenade, people would stop and point me out and say: 'Here comes Donna Laura, whom Petrarch loves. "You sweet fountain of Joy!",' they would shout after me. And another time: '"A lovelier foot has never trod the earth!,"' and everyone looked at my feet. And my Monsieur? He wavered between jealousy and vanity and the hope of some connection with the Pope's palace. He looked at me with new eyes; with your eyes.

Children painted my face on the gates of the house, the way children paint heads – lines and circles. Underneath was: Madonna Laura. I wore my hair hidden under a hood, but people knew: 'The golden tresses streaming in the breeze . . .'. When I went on my way to Santa Chiara, young girls would fall on their knees, sighing, and whispering: 'Madonna Laura!'

The whole of Avignon watched me. My Monsieur most of all. A poet was praising the beauty of his wife, and praising her virtue! He looked at me as at one of the statues at the portals

40

of the church. I had two admirers, but no husband any more and no lover!

I'm getting feverish again, Milli.

You write about tears. My tears flowed freely. You preserved yours in their little tear ducts under your eyes. Who for? In the meantime we grew old, Francesco. You saw my face in every cloud, in the branches of the trees, in the mist – Donna Laura was present everywhere. And you rode away. I learned of it from Carlo, who cooks for the Popes. You were in Rome – it was a question of crowning the poet with laurels. I was in Rome too, dwelling in your heart. All the same how I envied Milli her cook! I ought to have forbidden her to tell me all the things she told me. How she met him secretly in among the bushes on the riverbank, beneath the arches of the Pope's Palace. Her clothes were covered with flour. She brought me the sweet, bitter amaretti, nougat and candied fruits; the Lord High Cardinals loved sweetmeats. We nibbled and we whispered.

Milli! Are you asleep? Bring me a little nougat! Milli, can you hear me? Don't die before me! Oh – orange juice, from the bitter Seville oranges! Drink! You drink some too, Milli – drink from the same cup. Do you want to go on living then? Do you want to live longer than your mistress? Nobody will take you, you are half deaf. But we had some good times, didn't we? We used to laugh a lot? I used to watch you sweep the stairs. But I used to praise you too! You have served me faithfully – keep the cup! Wipe the sweat away! Bring me fresh sheets! Why don't you open the window?

What was I thinking about? We used to nibble Amaretti, those little, sweet cakes made from honey and ground almonds.

At table I got very little to eat. My Monsieur was of the opinion that it was not seemly for me to drink wine, or to enjoy any of the dishes that stood on the table in such abundance. I was supposed to stay pure and empty. Baron de Sade decided what was seemly.

In truth, it was Petrarch who determined my fate, just with words. He said: 'Her brow is pure!' And it was pure. He said: 'Her hair is golden!' And it was golden. You wrote about matrimony's tenacious bond. And what did you know about matrimony? It was all pure love on one hand and lusting after women on the other!

That other one showed herself quite brazenly, right in front of our house. She went about barefoot in wide skirts, and with her breasts bulging. She suckled your child under the arch in the gateway of our house and laughed. She laughed at me openly whenever I went by. I kept my eyes fixed on the ground, yet I saw everything! My eyes wouldn't shut tight any more, you had pierced them full of holes. They said that you lived with her in Vaucluse, near some spring, that you called 'Queen of the Springs'. I had to endure her mockery. I had to share you with her. The part of you I possessed meant nothing to her. My breasts, which nobody saw, shrivelled away because no one fondled them. Milli used to stuff silk kerchiefs into my bodice.

You fobbed me off with words. I carried them with me everywhere I went. You plucked the flowers and the grasses where my feet had trodden. You celebrated the branch which I had clung to for support; the meadows full of flowers, where I would rest; the blossoms that dropped onto my hair; and you wrote: they 'shimmered like pearls and like gold'. Where were the flowery meadows? Where was the tree? You were dreaming, Petrarch; and you taught me to dream as well. I asked my husband for a piece of Lyons silk, and I asked for yarns and threads. I described to him the colours that I needed: olive-green, lavender-blue, greeny-orange and also pink. Then I began to sew.

What is Madonna Laura doing?

She is doing her embroidery.

I was embroidering the tapestry of my life. For one whole year I embroidered nothing but lavender. I spent another year on a stone pine. Oh, and that summer embroidering the yellow gorse! But of course, the orange tree on my tapestry bears no fruit. The oranges lie in the grass under the tree, as if the wind had gathered them. There is no fruit hanging on the olive tree, which was the first thing I embroidered; every single one is lying in the grass. It's the same with the fig tree; and nothing that has once borne fruit is still in blossom. Who can read the tapestry? My Monsieur, when he returned from his travels, brought back threads of spun gold; I thanked him. Even he hasn't seen my tapestry; has never asked to see it. He was anxious that I should not run out of yarn, so that I would stay in my room, sewing, and not notice anything of the dissolute life in Avignon. He would accompany me to church, and wait while I made my confession. What should I have confessed? My brow was pure; and, later on, even my thoughts were, too. I had become what Petrarch had foreseen: pure. For two years I stitched away at a windmill. It had white sails and strong stone walls. It took another half a year to remove the sails, to unpick the threads. The white sails didn't fit into the picture. You strung words together to make a sentence. I took threads. Where you put a full stop, I made a little knot. No one will realise that I have concealed your face in a laurel tree. The craggy forehead, the bold nose, the powerful chin.

After that first glance in Santa Chiara we never dared to look at each other again. I would turn my head to one side, so that you could look at me, and you did the same. I arranged the branches of the laurel tree, so that one branch covered your forehead. You went to Rome that year and were crowned by others. The greatest poet in the land of poets! You wrote: 'Ah, you are everywhere!', and rode away and took me with you: and in spite of that I sat here by the window and went on embroidering. You wrote poems as if you were whispering in my ear, you were so close! I felt your breath. Your hand, caressing the page as if it were my cheek. With one stroke of your quill you pushed aside mountains and oceans. Anyone who can read, can read what you write. No one ever entered my chamber except Milli, and she would issue bulletins: 'Madonna Laura is embroidering a laurel bush now!' When I went for a walk in the afternoon, in the shade of the plane trees, accompanied by Monsieur, there would be a whispering: 'Now she's embroidering a laurel bush!' Milord de Sade found it flattering. He found his consolation in another house.

When Milli wanted to tell me her latest about her cook, I forbade her to talk. I said: 'Be silent! You are offending my ears!' Then she pushed aside my hood and gazed at my ear and said: 'It is so rosy and beautiful, just like Petrarch says.' I said: 'Don't touch my hood!' When she wanted to wash my hair, I said: 'It isn't necessary, last night I was walking up and down in the rain.' The truth is, I have torn my hair out, hair by hair. I used my hair to embroider your head. My head is bald.

Come closer, Milli! Listen! Before they stick me in one of those barrels, you must wrap me up in my tapestry. Has milord de Sade already seen to a barrel? Bind my chin up with my veil, so that the piece of gold doesn't fall out of my mouth. Why are you crying, Milli? Hasn't there been enough crying in this house? Give me some wine! I'm getting all confused.

When my Monsieur sat opposite me at table drinking wine, while I drank water, he said: 'In Venice they talk about Dante and Beatrice; but in Avignon, and soon throughout the country, they will talk about Petrarch and Laura! Love has a new name – called Donna Laura!'

He was intoxicated, not just with the wine, he was drunk with his own vanity. He, who had hardly ever spoken with me, was saying what I knew, what everyone knows. He spoke about the active life, of the life of the senses, and of the contemplative life, and he took the celebrated Petrarch as his example: he observes the way the world wags; he thinks, he writes. I smiled. That was enough of an answer for him. I didn't ask which kind of life he thought his own belonged to. And mine.

You don't pick the figs, Petrarch, you just look at them, think about them, praise their sweetness and their bloom. Was I the fig that was ripening on the tree and now grows rotten and falls?

They say you are weary of the world, Francesco; that you are sunk deep in gloom. You are sick of life; I am dying of the plague! I wanted to go just one more time to Santa Chiara, the few steps. I could have held on to the walls of the houses for support. They pray there for the sick. But my door is guarded. I fell down in a swoon. My body was lying there in front of the door. Milli pushed me back to my couch with her feet. Then she crossed herself and lifted me up. She is suffering with her mistress but she doesn't want to die with her. She recoils in disgust from this body, whose praises she used to sing because it was as white as milk. The Black Death. I sink down into dreams and then I surface again.

Francesco! These thighs, that you never knew, are covered with boils, as big as quails' eggs. There is pus oozing from my armpits. Milli burns the sheets in the courtyard and the smoke rises up straight as an arrow, pitch black. She burns wormwood leaves in my chamber. When I was young she would put sprigs of fresh wormwood under my pillows so I would be able to bear milord de Sade's nightly visit more easily. So that I would feel passion. And later, when he began to stay away, my husband, then she would make me tea from wormwood, mixed with poppyseed. I would drink the tea and grow sleepy. When the nights were hot, she would give me fresh cool sheets, and she would close the shutters so that the moon wouldn't make me restless.

My tongue is becoming heavy, I am babbling. Set fire to the house, Milli, let me burn away!

Your immortal beloved is dying, Petrarch, your saint! Ah! If only you had loved me as a mortal being, Petrarch. Your mind was fixed on immortal things. You were not weeping over me, you were weeping over your own pain. You didn't love me, you loved the love you felt for me. When I am dead, you will still see me in every cloud, in every laurel. The soft wind will take my voice to waft words of tenderness into your yearning ears. Ah! I have learnt to speak after your fashion, to sigh sighs, to suffer pain, and to love love.

Have I really lived?

Did you just invent me?

# *An octave lower, please,*

# *Fräulein von Meysenbug!*

A discourse directed by

the incensed

Christine Brückner to

von Meysenbug,

her co-utopian

# Malvida von Meysenbug

*Malvida von Meysenbug was born in Kassel, in the region of Hesse, in 1816, into an aristocratic family of partly French origin. She declared her solidarity with the revolutionaries of 1848, and in 1852 was forced to leave her home in Berlin, because of her many connections with democratic thinkers and politicians. She went first to England, where she was governess to the young daughter of Alexander Herzen, and then to Italy. She settled there in 1862 and died in Rome in 1903. She wrote at least one novel, stories and several books of memoirs in which she recalls some of the friendships which in the end form her chief claim to fame, with among others, Nietzsche, Wagner, Garibaldi, Mazzini, Liszt and Schopenhauer.*

# An octave lower, please, Fräulein von Meysenbug!

A discourse directed by the incensed Christine Brückner
to von Meysenbug, her co-utopian

My dear Fräulein von Meysenbug!
You called your recollections – not without a certain self-
glorification – *The Memoirs of an Idealist*, and dedicated them
to those fortunate sisters who were able to grow up breathing the
free air of unassailable rights. From time to time I shall permit
myself to address you as 'sister' in return. I am just such a more
fortunate sister, and I want to thank you for some of those things
– not all! – that you have contributed towards the emancipation
of women.

You regarded yourself as an idealist, but you were really
a fantasist. A dreamer. You write that you trod the narrow
path of the lone soul, looking up to the stars, and not
at the shining brightness of ballroom chandeliers. This
lonely path just happened to be swarming with artists,
philosophers, theologians . . . Under your name the Grosse

Brockhaus encyclopaedia lists several celebrities: Richard Wagner, Friedrich Nietzsche, Romain Rolland and, so it says, other of the leading spirits of Europe. The greatest composer of your time, the greatest philosopher of your time, one of the great literary figures of your time; the princesses and the cardinals don't get so much as a mention.

Wherever you went your way was smoothed for you, my dear Malvida, by your aristocratic name, your careful upbringing, your artistic leanings. You couldn't help those? I am not reproaching you with your antecedents. But neither do I leave them out of account.

You spent your childhood in a distinguished house. Your father was a Minister in the Elector's court at Kassel. You got to know the drawbacks, but also the advantages of court life. You broke free only with difficulty from your family ties, and earned your own living only because you didn't want to live in material dependency upon those from whom you had freed your spirit, and who did not share your progressive views. You arrived at your own conclusions, based on theory, as to how we should conduct ourselves. You – an aristocrat by birth and upbringing – became a democrat by conviction. That was very noble. You hold the opinion that we may accept material sacrifice only from those with whom we find ourselves in full spiritual accord; and that we may not claim support from those upon whom, because of our own convictions, we have inflicted bitter hurt. What demands you do make upon mankind! Upon mankind – well, that would be all right; but such demands on the individual! Today, my dear sister, it is customary to make claims not first of all upon oneself, but upon others: on society, on the state. Especially on the state!

That does not mean, of course, that one may not criticise the state. You think that out of the question? An example: You knew

Georg Büchner? His *Hessian Courier*? Or his drama, *Danton's Death*? Büchner was obliged to quit the country of Hesse, accused of treacherous intrigue against the state. He espoused radical political views much as you did. He went to Alsace, you fled from Berlin to England. He too evaded arrest through flight.

Today, a much sought-after literary prize has been named after this revolutionary writer. For preference it is bestowed on rebellious poets; and these accept the prize, albeit from time to time with some scruples, and at the prize-giving ceremony they speak their mind – to the donor of the prize, the state of Hesse – without pulling their punches. The state rewards its rebels! Do you recognise progress? Today everyone can revile the state and still remain in its service. It is the custom to separate speaking, thinking and writing from the way you act! You became aware that governments could be dispensed with in a whole range of matters. You even use the word 'superfluous' in this connection. My foolish sister! Today the state is called on more than ever before. 'State responsibility' – that has become a byword. It's the state that has duties towards its citizens, who for their part must pay the state taxes. Citizens have legitimate claims; they are entitled to some return for their money. If a government doesn't fulfil their claims they won't elect it again. In the meantime we have universal suffrage: the right to vote, not the duty to vote. How you do go on in your writing about duties!

You were of the opinion that the world had not yet arrived at the limits of knowledge; that progress was continuing; that – and this was your comfort – the development of life was unending. Death was only the transition to another form of being; and perhaps the atoms which once formed a poet's brow, an uplifted heart, might reappear in a fragrant blossom and from there continue their migration into new human forms, and that the glorious thoughts which sprang from that brow, the love which impelled that heart to acts of comfort and compassion, might find themselves intertwined in the immortality of the fountain of life, which inspires man after man and generation after generation to goodness, greatness and beauty.

My dear sister and colleague, please don't play with your foot on the pedal the whole time! One octave lower, if I may make so bold! Did you really believe all that? Did you know no doubts? What happened to your sense of humour, your irony? All admiration, you reiterate Goethe's demand that man be noble, generous, and good. I too count as a moralist, but I'm not at all sure of my ground – I often have a good laugh at myself. The words that you are constantly repeating are: justice, independence, progress. Yes – progress above all. Today we encompass all these concepts in the words 'equal opportunity'. I do not – you must believe me! – doubt the truthfulness of your ideals! You yourself came very close to your own goals. You achieved success as a writer – at the time you were more famous than Nietzsche. You, who in your young days admired others were, later, yourself the object of admiration. You were able to live in Italy, the land of your dreams. You are buried in one of the most beautiful cemeteries in the world, in Rome, close to the Cestius-Pyramid. I have stood at your graveside. Sunlight filtered through pine trees and cypresses. I was impressed by your famous neighbours. Goethe's son, the poets Shelley and Keats . . . You, the atheist, who prided yourself on not belonging to any orthodox community but to that great community of those who love the Good, the Lofty and the Beautiful, and strive to realise it within and around themselves, you now lie in a cemetery where the words 'Resurrecturis' – 'To those who shall rise again' – stand above the entrance. That, surely, was not what you had in mind.

Would you agree with me, were I to maintain that good fortune is made possible only by injustice? You were born a privileged woman. You died a privileged woman. At the cost of others. You took a few steps along the road to emancipation. The idea of leading women to complete freedom of spiritual development, to economic independence and to the possession of all the rights of citizenship, has been widely realised. Women have the same right to develop their potential through instruction and study as men; women have been freed from the 'yoke of ignorance, superstition, frivolity and fashion'. Or have they? In the interim, women's path has taken quite another direction. What concerns us more today are general social questions. The goals have become littler. They have to do with examination results, material benefits in old age, equal pay, abortion. The big goals, which touched on one's own inner self, the 'I' and the 'we' and the perfectibility of the world, have been lost from view along the way.

The world has not changed in the way you meant it to. You and your friends were striving towards perfection of the soul and of the spirit. Today the striving is towards perfect standards of living, perfect cars, bathrooms, nurseries, flawless make-up. What you were afraid of, at the end of your long life, has come to pass: material considerations have gained power over mankind. Today when we speak of progress, which we do almost as often as you did then, we mean above all, technical progress; in that sphere, what we have accomplished is astounding; as it is in the social realm. You were obliged to resort to servants, whose spiritual ignorance and economic dependency you so deeply lamented. We modern women don't allow ourselves to be waited on any more. We make use of all kinds of household machines, which we operate on our own, and the servants of yore now work

53

in factories, on what are called assembly lines. We continue to use the word 'dependency', and words like 'contingent' and 'related', especially in connection with wages, as in 'wage-related'. These working women are unionised. Working hours, leisure hours, maternity pay, redundancy pay, Christmas bonus, unemployment benefit – it is all laid down in strict accordance with an agreed wage scale; and it is still being perfected.

Please excuse me, dear Fräulein von Meysenbug, if I go on yet again about material things. But even they represent a kind of progress! Today every man and every woman, or almost every man and almost every woman, can travel to places where formerly only the privileged could travel. For example, to the Mediterranean coast, to the island of Ischia. You wouldn't feel at home there any more; it's teeming with tourists spending two weeks' holiday, where you used to be able to spend months in longed-for solitude and serendipitous society. It was a happy accident that all your friends owned beautiful summer residences in beautiful countryside, on the English coast as well as on the lakes of Northern Italy. You could stay there as a guest for weeks on end.

'Oui, c'était quelqu'un!' as you used to put it. 'Yes – he was really *somebody*!' With ordinary mortals, you seem to have come into contact very seldom – and only then as benefactress. Presumably, a hundred years later, you would have sat with Sartre in the 'Café aux deux Magots', and been in and out of the Karajans' house; but in order to do that, my dear, you would have had to be – and to stay – very young and very beautiful. Who, today, would have been worthy of your admiration and your friendship? Would you have appeared on a talk show with the theologian Hans Küng, to discuss religious questions? I look at your picture and ask myself whether you would have appealed to Picasso. I ask myself, moreover, whether the famous men of my time would have flown along with your soaring of soul and spirit. Have tastes changed? At all events, the demands that men make on women have altered. During the Third Reich you would have had to emigrate because of your socialist ideas. Perhaps you would even have reached the haven of the United States of America? To go to free America was certainly one of your life's unfulfilled ambitions. (You would not have needed to show any consideration for the feelings of your parents in our century, of that I can assure you.) Perhaps you would have lived in the same neighbourhood as Thomas Mann, with a view of the Pacific. He would not have failed to record his impressions of the idealist MvM in his diary, with engaging sharpness.

I try to imagine you conducting frequent and vital telephone conversations with Heinrich Böll, relieving him of part of the burden – thrust upon him – of being the conscience of the Nation. Probably you, the revolutionary of 1848, would have been sympathetic to our young student rebels of 1968. For you were impatient also, wanted to realise your goals quickly. And today too, a house raid, like the one before your flight from Berlin, could not be completely ruled out.

One of your large ideas I find very pleasing, though I should never dare to express it. You considered it to be conceivable and reasonable that the ownership of property cease with the death of the person who acquired it. Each individual would have to buckle down to work, and a great many iniquities which arise from laziness induced by inherited wealth would be prevented. It's an illuminating thought, but I don't for a moment consider that it is feasible. Today too, the only people who want to share are those who would profit from the sharing out of possessions, not those who own the things that can be shared.

Dear sister, does my prosaic outlook get on your nerves? Your relentless idealism has the same effect on me. For example you argue for Art as a means of perfecting mankind to the highest degree. According to your conception, the noblest works of art should be offered so cheaply that even those who don't own a thing can have a share in them, and may in that way be led along the path of culture. Those are the real cultural obligations of Government. Great Art might be able to work more effectively against brutality and crime than prisons and prison cells. How can I make you understand, dear Fräulein von Meysenbug? The treatment of prisoners has become more humane, but it just isn't possible to send the occupants of penal institutions to the Bayreuth or the Salzburg Festival. Because of the relatively small scale of the set-up only a select circle can take part in the Bayreuth Festival. There is no doubt that this need for the appreciation of Art exists – it represents one of the great social phenomena; but for those poor people to whom you – who were able to attend the first performances at the Master's side – were kind enough to turn your thoughts again and again, the cost of a ticket is too high.

I permit myself to dub you 'the friend of significant men'. You preferred friendship with many men to loving only one. Dear Malvida! You begin to spook me a little! How did you manage to keep on admiring these men? Could you only keep the friendships going, through unremitting admiration? I have taken the trouble of collecting together the adjectives which the biographers of these great personalities have conferred on you. Clever Malvida; the understanding friend; the discreet counsellor; the truest, most helpful friend, the mediator in differences and quarrels . . . Your calming influence was famous. You lent your counsel to the dying Wagner, and to the dying Princess Wittgenstein, too. You must have been a wonderfully balanced woman. Throughout the course of your life there was never a hint of gossip. Could there have been a touch of the Victorian prude about you? When your first love remained unfulfilled did you, more and more, become a sexless being? Your view is that love for a man, even love for a child, turns a woman into a slave. You write that in old age sex, with all its delights, must clearly become disgusting, since its purpose – the propagation of the species – can no longer be attained. The compensation for old age, therefore, is sexlessness – the respite from desire, the approach to pure spirituality, the second maidenhead of the soul. Dear sister-in-sex, I am of another opinion – I am all for Love! You were transported to your seventh heaven when you read Schopenhauer. *I* tried it. I read a few pages of his masterpiece *The World as Will and Idea* . . . I didn't experience any comparable transports.

When you saw prostitutes in Hamburg and most of all, later, in London, it affected you deeply and made you very angry. These unhappy souls were obliged to pay a tax to the state in order to be allowed to practise their hideous vocation! In this area a lot has changed. Now one sees the poor creatures on the streets only rarely; and they are not really poor creatures, far from it – their incomes are good to very good. For the most part these women have apartments; customers are recruited just as with other advertising, by giving out a few relevant details in the news-paper: first name, colour of hair, bust measurement. The tax authorities have not yet satisfactorily worked out what share of the incomes from this profession can be claimed by the state.

Granting to the body its right to joy means taking joy away from the spirit! Is that really your view, my dear colleague? A recent poll revealed that life's highest pleasures are produced by Sex, as we call it. So far there has not been an opinion poll on the joys of the spirit. Lately an enquiry conducted among students showed that those who are sexually satisfied achieve a better performance intellectually. So there seems in your case to have been some sort of repression at work. There has always been repression. Today it is ideals which are repressed. We use the word 'ideal' in another sense. For instance we speak of the ideal body. Prizes are awarded for male and female beauty.

You complain that you will have to take with you to the grave the hope that woman would no longer be a doll or a slave, but that she would stand beside man as an aware and free being, and work with him towards the perfection of life in the family, in society, in the state, in Art; towards the realisation of the Ideal in the life of humankind. I suspect, dear colleague, that, just like you, I will take this hope – yes, it is my hope, too, though I express it differently – to the grave with me. A glance at the magazine covers on a newspaper kiosk would bring a blush to your cheek; or ought I to say, would cause you to turn pale? (You have never expressed yourself on the subject of your physical reactions.) Rich men are still acquiring young and lovely women for themselves like so many pieces of jewellery. Women use their exposed bodies like billboards for the purpose of promoting their wares, and thereby demonstrate their newly won freedom. Nowadays we talk quite openly about sexuality. It is one of the main themes, for both male and female writers; and for the readers too, of course. In every class of society, there is the same degree of interest in this subject. Sexuality demonstrably existed, even in your century, and human beings have not altered essentially since, nor have they attained perfection. The changes are to be found in the social sphere. Of their own free will many couples live together in unlicensed association. Presumably such a liaison, which is founded on independence and self-reliance, would please you. Sadly, however, this form of living together is not any guarantee of happiness either; the decisive factors are not, as a rule, idealistic but material ones.

Many times, my honoured sister, you have expressed the opinion that women should not become like men; they should not imitate man's brutality but should help him to free himself from all wickedness, in readiness for the great cultural work of mankind. You wanted to augment the worth of women and mothers through the development of their intellectual abilities, in order that they might be not only the procreators but also the educators of youth. How am I to interpret that? That a woman should have no career of her own? What should this comprehensively educated woman do, when her children have grown up and left the parental home? Concern herself exclusively with refining her husband? Work free and gratis towards the perfecting of humanity? Renounce all personal income, any thought of her own car, her own bank account, of taking herself off to foreign parts? Your equations don't work out. Once again, I am obliged to water your pure wine. The economic independence of women is the very thing you so often extolled. In fact, as regards economics, we have come a very great deal further.

You wanted to set a noble and natural check to man's brutal sex drive, as you call it, through intensified education and increasing the capacity for intellectual output, so that fewer and nobler examples of the human species would be produced. The finest types would have to get together . . . At this point I broke off from my reading. Listen to me, Fräulein von Meysenbug! Your views are élitist! What you are suggesting there is genetic engineering!

You attempt to justify yourself by referring to the Greek gods, who are supposed to have sought commerce with the noblest mortals. Your ideas were taken up in the so-called Thousand Year Reich which, to be sure, only lasted twelve. That's pure Nietzsche! There have been just such establishments for breeding men of exceptional racial worth. I venture to doubt whether the results would have lived up to your expectations. And as far as men's brutal sex drive is concerned, in this day and age that has certainly been brought under control – we call it birth control.

I know your objections! Nature herself is aristocratic. She is sparing with the best organisms in the plant and animal world, just as she is with the great spiritual giants among human beings. Whereas she is all extravagance with the masses, as if it mattered to her not a jot that thousands perish without ever experiencing even for a moment what it is to be like the Gods. And in spite of that, my dear, you demand progress for all?

Today we have decided against the aristocratic principle of predetermined endowment in favour of the democratic principle. Everyone is urged forward whether they want to be or not. We offer young people of both sexes equality of opportunity, and seek thereby to restore the balance created by the injustices of nature and heredity. Everyone can make claims, on parents, on schools, on church and state. Everyone has the right to every right! Did you really assume that individuals must first of all make claims upon themselves? That one must ask first about duties, and only then about rights?

You are hopelessly Utopian! Allow one of those fortunate sisters to say that to you – she's a Utopian too.

# Don't forget the kingfisher's name

Sappho bids farewell

to the young girls

leaving Lesbos

# Sappho

*The great Greek poetess was born at the beginning of the sixth century BC in Lesbos. Little is known about her but it is thought that she was married and had at least one daughter. She followed the fashion of the time in gathering a group of young women around her, possibly in a form of religious association for the worship of the goddess Aphrodite, possibly simply for the leisured pursuit of writing and discussing poetry and literature. Her own poetry is intense and personal, concerning her feelings towards her family and, still more, towards her group of girls, whom she addresses in tones that vary from affection to passionate love. The source and authenticity of the story of her own unrequited passion for Phaon are uncertain. His own story is the stuff of legend, as he was an old and rather ugly boatman, who is said one day to have ferried the goddess Aphrodite across the sea. He refused to accept any payment and the goddess rewarded him by granting him youth and beauty. It is after this that Sappho is supposed to have fallen for him, both metaphorically and literally – when he spurned her she is said to have hurled herself from the cliff-top of the Leucadian promontory.*

# *Don't forget the*
# *kingfisher's name*

### Sappho bids farewell to the
### young girls leaving Lesbos

How lovely you are – my girls! I taught you how to weave the crowns of flowers that adorn your hair today. Dancing with feet as light as gossamer to do the Goddess honour. Your voices ring out as bright and clear as the song of the lark rising in the morning. Don't look back! I taught you to be happy and to make others happy. I stand in the shadows – all the light is falling on you. You are my work, I sacrifice you to the Goddess Aphrodite – I give you up. I have prepared you ill for your roles as wives. Forgive me. By this evening a man's hand will already be tangled in Dika's hair. This very day your husbands will be undoing the ribbons which I taught you how to tie with such artistry; and you will minister to their raging desires, obey their exigent voices. Happy the man who will call you his own; unhappy, she whom you are forsaking.

I loved you all. Loved all of you in one of you; loved in you

– and honoured – Aphrodite, the Goddess of Love, of Youth, of Beauty. Come! Gather around me once again, place me in your midst, conceal my ageing body from the eyes of the Goddess. Girls – Oh do not weep! I can see your arms stretching out toward the man to whom henceforward you will belong. But do not forget the Gardens of Mytelene; do not forget Sappho! You have been used to freedom – to days passed in play and in dancing. You have been told that this day, today, is the most beautiful and most important day of your life – you believed it, because everyone believes it. I have not taught you the art of suffering and enduring. I have kept from you what it is that awaits you. Sorrows are waiting for you. Duties! No longer will you detect the call of the nightjar, because a man will lie beside you on your couch – snoring, after taking too much wine. And in the mornings it is no longer the call of the finch that will waken you, but your wailing child, whose first tooth is on its way. I forgot to tell you about teething. Our lavishness will be a thing of the past; you will have to learn thrift; the talk will be all of rancid oil, nothing of the deep shade spreading under the olive tree. Take care to see that the water jugs are always full. Send the maids to the spring, but don't forget how you used to look at your own reflections and bathe in the fountain.

Don't forget the kingfisher's name! You spoke the words in chorus and the words turned into songs. Aphrodite passed among you and leaned, smiling, against the trunk of the flowering pomegranate tree. Everything was blossom and springtime and desire. I never told you that it all passes. You lived a today that had no end. The days were gifts that we gave away. Naked and barefoot you walked over the grass with steps so light they seemed to skim each blade. You learned to destroy nothing of all that the Gods let grow. With what tender solicitude you lifted up the snails and set them down again on the edges of the paths! Not one of you ever did any harm to the little lizard. Now you will have to take the quail's warm little body in your hands and wring its neck, pluck off its feathers, tear out its entrails. I have kept that from you. Your husband's mother is only waiting for the moment when she can teach you how to kill with a steady hand.

In the first hour of the day, when night was still lying in the valleys, and as yet only the mountains were lit up by the beams of the rising sun, I got up and cut a rose and placed it upon Dika, who was my favourite. Drops of dew fell from the rose onto her dreaming face, an augury of tears. I let the night go by, waiting for the morning; I lay without sleeping. While you were all asleep, looking forward towards life, I lay watching with a view of death. I betrayed nothing to you – nothing of the loneliness, nothing. I was a tree, you were the leaves. I taught you to identify every fragrance, named the names of the plants for you, and the constellations. You played the flute and the lyre, sang songs. The breezes carried the notes and the words to you. I would say: 'Sing what you see! Play what you hear!' I wrote upon the leaves and tore the leaves up and scattered them in the wind. A poem is like a tree that covers itself in greenery and then throws its leaves away when the autumn comes. You forget and you will be forgotten. My songs murmured into the rosy shells of your ears like the waves of the sea, and the waves of the sea will bring my songs back to you when you are old; when you remember the belovèd grove of apple trees beneath which we used to rest, side by side, breathing the scent of honey. Aphrodite was your mistress; from now on Hera, the Goddess of fertility, will be your mistress; to whom I now must deliver you up — to my sorrow.

More than the beauty of boys, I loved the beauty of young women, who carry their sex hidden within them. How could I compare beauty with beauty! Love does not make comparisons. Tender days. My hand would slide so lightly over Abanthis's glowing body. To be beautiful and graceful for Aphrodite — that was your goal, when you adorned yourselves, when you wove crowns from the pungent aniseed flower and crowned each other with them! Abanthis's curls lay upon her shoulders with hues of melted gold like the locks of Apollo.

You were accustomed to freedom — were like the birds that chatter and sing, and refresh themselves at the fountain and sleep at night among the green branches. Tomorrow they will lock you in cages. You will become domestic animals; you will stop singing. Don't believe them, whatever promises they make! Today they shower you with gifts. But are you not beautiful enough? Why do they put chains on your arms, slide rings on to your fingers? They will shroud your young girls' heads beneath the kerchief of the married woman. Dika! Gongyla! Abanthis! When you arrayed yourselves in your festal garments, and raised your sweet voices; when you leaped over the rocks, each one of you was like a demi-goddess. I shall call out your names and the waves will swallow up the sound of my sorrowing voice. And then I shall submit myself to the will of the Gods. If, yesterday, I still loved Athis, tomorrow I shall love Anaktoria. If I felt longing yesterday, so today I must suffer the pangs of separation. Always the same wild feelings. A love-vessel which overflows and which, when it is empty, has to charge itself afresh, like a water-butt in the winter rain.

I taught you tenderness; you discovered your bodies before any man discovered them. Dika, you have let me sense that my caress was not enough any more – that you are hankering after other pleasures. My songs were meant for you Dika, my smile for you; you knew it, and would wriggle your toes, and it was a sign meant for me, and made me happy. Women's love is more reticent than men's. Ageing men, on the street and in the squares, move about freely with the boy of their choice; teacher and pupil. Both strive to distinguish themselves, so as to bring honour and joy to the other. Youth and age belong together; they have to separate and find each other again, to change rôles. Later you yourselves will be a Sappho, and teach young girls, and everything will flow forward in the river of time.

I like to listen to the shrewd old men, to contemplate their faces, which bear the marks of sweat and tears. I can see past hardships and sorrows still to come. Their wrists are furrowed by the bracelets of time, and unsightly liverspots dull their skins. In my songs the name of Kerkylas, who was my husband, who wanted to rule me, is nowhere to be found. Saying nothing is worse than saying things that are unkind. I have forgotten the joys and the pains that men afford us. A man made me the mother of my daughter, Kléis, whom I had to give up to a man, as now I must give you up. My words perish in the songs that I have taught you to sing. You are forsaking me – but Eros remains to me.

Wisdom is the beauty that belongs to age. When you grow old, think then of Sappho, who was old when you were young. You will still find joy in the sun that warms you; joy in gardens; in reflections glittering on the waves. Women love the things that abide. Men love anything that can carry them away; they love horses, and they love ships. There are girls growing up every year – take pleasure in them and give them pleasure.

Soon I shall adorn myself for the last journey across Acheron. If there were anything beautiful about dying the Gods would not be immortal. They would live in Hades and stay there and never come back to Earth. When I stood on the Leucadian cliff, my feet wanted to jump but my hands clung fast, clawing at the rocks. The frail stalks of Dill sufficed to hold me. Must I wait, then, for Charon to fetch me? Why do I not, of my own free will, do what must, surely, be done?

Will Old Age twist me and bow me down? Will my mind lose its way? Will my voice begin to babble? Oh you Gods! What will become of Sappho? Who will take me by the hand when I leap towards death? Can the happiness of bygone days no longer warm me? Have I ceased to be Sappho, the poetess of Lesbos, celebrated everywhere? Must I sink back into the chorus of wailing women.

Ah!

I love young Phaon! To have him – I would have given all of you up; all of you; all my girls!

# 'So I was Goethe's other – fatter – half?'

Christiane von Goethe
in the ante-chamber of
Frau Charlotte von Stein,
widow of the late
Master of the Duke's Horse

# Christiane von Goethe

*Christiane von Goethe was born Christiane Vulpius, daughter of a lowly official in Weimar, capital of the German province of Thuringia. Johann Wolfgang von Goethe (1749–1832), who was to become one of the true giants of world literature and thought, had already achieved great fame at twenty-five, through his novel* Werther, *though he had trained and practised as a lawyer. In 1775 he came to Weimar, where he lived for the rest of his life, and took up a post in the service of the duke. He fell in love with Charlotte von Stein, the wife of the Master of the Duke's Horse. She was several years his senior, a woman of fine intellect and considerable social sophistication. She became his mentor as well as his passion but insisted that their relationship remain purely platonic. In 1786 feeling stifled by the constraints of Weimar society Goethe set off abruptly for Italy, spent two years there, and was revitalised by the change of scene and perspectives. The Roman Elegies, a series of lyrical, erotic poems which he wrote in 1788, are a celebration of his life with Christiane whom he met on his return from Rome. She not only became Goethe's mistress but lived with him openly and bore him several children. Weimar society was scandalised by the relationship, all the more because of Christiane's humble origins and lack of breeding. In 1806, when their lives and property were jeopardised by the invading French, he married her.*

# 'So I was Goethe's
# other – fatter – half?'

Christiane von Goethe in the ante-chamber of Frau Charlotte
von Stein – widow of the late Master of the Duke's Horse

The Frau Oberstallmeisterin is not receiving? She is not feeling
herself? Well, that's all right. I can wait. Perhaps she will be
feeling herself again shortly? I might as well take a seat. Perhaps
sometime she'll have to leave her Salon and come through the
lobby, and who should be sitting there but the former Miss
Vulpius, as was? Nobody can get past her now, Madame von Stein,
not even you. Should I speak louder, so that you can understand
me? Or are you stopping up your ears because I talk so common?
Thuringian! You talk the same yourself, only more stuck-up.

I can't fit into your armchair, I'm too broad in the beam. You're
obviously not meant to make yourself too comfy here, then?
You've got to squeeze your knees up tight and sit bolt upright.
Definitely no lolling. But I like to take it easy wherever I am.
And now I'm really having a good old sprawl – only because that's
what you expect.

Is the port wine for me? Or is it supposed to be for other visitors as well? Who else can be coming? The people of Weimar are all frightened of your sharp tongue. Did you have the decanter filled up when you saw the carriage of that Vulpius woman drive up to the door? Do you want to see if I empty the decanter? Well, Madame, that depends how long you keep me waiting. Who has more patience.

Now you're curious to know whether My Own One knows I'm paying you a visit. He happens, currently, to be on his travels, as everyone in Weimar knows, and you know too. And when he comes back he'll tell me how it all was, and I'll tell him how it was in Weimar: and perhaps I'll tell him also that Frau von Stein wasn't feeling herself and couldn't receive poor, ailing Frau von Goethe. I thought us might have a few things to say to each other. When the end is in sight then it's time to put an end to quarrels as well. We ought to set things to rights, between us. Perhaps there've been one or two things said you'd be only too happy to take back? Words can weigh heavy. You've given orders that, when the time comes, your coffin-bearers are not to carry your corpse round by way of the Frauenplan. If it's on my account you can spare yourself the detour: I'll be on my way before you, Madame! And My Own One won't be standing at the window either – he steers clear of death.

I'll help myself to another, if that's permitted. And now, I'll tell you how it all came about. I never wanted anything for myself from Herr von Goethe. I was only handing him over a petition from my brother. All he did was just look at me, and I curtsied and went bright red and I laughed – because a poor girl can't afford to be proud. He invited me to his gardenhouse. At first people just thought, young Miss Vulpius cooks and cleans for him, nothing more to it. But the 'nothing more' was the most important thing. For him I wasn't just a female hand at the Bertusch factory, making artificial flowers; for him I was a flower-girl. I was his girl. He loved girls. He had enough of Ladies!

I used to creep in secretly through the garden, round the back way. The weir by the River Ilm always made such a roar, so no one ever heard me. He didn't want to be talked about, and I wasn't to be talked about either. But in Weimar, everyone's got three eyes and three ears! When they twigged that I was with him day and night – then suddenly: I was a little guttersnipe! I was a whore. My family was common as muck. My father was a drunkard.

But My Own One gave me a key and said: 'To our wee little house . . .' I hacked and weeded and fetched water from the River Ilm and watered the flowers and they grew and filled the air with their sweet scent. That's what I liked most, being out of doors among flowers that had thorns, and wilted: not like the silk flowers that I used to have to make at Bertusch's, for fine ladies like you. When us heard that the wife of the Herr Oberstallmeister wore our flowers on her bosom, us girls was that proud; 'her imposing bosom . . .' us used to call it.

Whenever My Own One went to Jena for a few days and I was alone in the wee little house, I would make myself useful; and when he came back I wasn't ever cross and I never asked 'How was it?' and 'Where have you been?' Then we'd have our canoodling sessions – he was as keen on them as I was. His mother in Frankfurt, the Frau Councillor, called him her cuddlehead and he liked a cuddle, and me too. And without mentioning my name, he sang my praises. He said that now he had a house and good things to eat and drink, and so on and so forth, and people knew what he meant by 'and so on and so forth' and they whispered and tut-tutted and I didn't dare venture out into the street.

But the way he saw it: us knew in us hearts us was married, us just hadn't been through the ceremony. It had not been his lot to see that many good marriages – not in Weimar and not in Jena either. And not one that had given him the urge to follow suit. They were all to do with rank and respectability – nothing to do with fun, and having a laugh.

I never had much learning – only enough to read and write, but I kept my eyes and ears open, and my thoughts used to run after his thoughts and turn complete somersaults and often never got there at all. He used to read what he wrote out loud to me, not just to you, Madame; and he still does today, sometimes. And I'd listen and nod and laugh, and cry my eyes out, if it was sad. And if it was boring I fell asleep. I was like the Public. And you were his critic. No one wants to be criticised in his own home. That's where he wants to be loved and looked up to. And mostly it would end with us letting our hair down and having a bit of a time of it! You don't know what that is? Didn't you and the Herr Oberstallmeister ever do that? I'm not saying what! Besides, it's not the sort of thing you'd have much call to know any more anyway.

So. What did you tell your maidservant when she spotted that 'Vulpius woman' through the peep-hole? 'I am not at home to milady Vulpius'? 'I am unwell. Indisposed'? Does the sight of me make you feel poorly? There's a funny smell here, Madame – sour; as soon as you come up the stairs. Never gets properly aired. I come from humble stock, out of the gutter, or however you like to put it. But now I've made my way in life – without my ever meaning to, it just happened – I say to the coachman: 'Have the goodness to drive me to Frau Oberstallmeisterin von Stein. No need to wait, there are some things us has to talk about – it will take some time.'

Now I see it with my own eyes. You live like a church mouse. The floorboards creak. No carpets left. No chandeliers. No upholstery on the chairs . . . But a silver salver for visiting cards! And you sit at the window and peer into the street to see what mistakes people are making, and sneer at them. You are an onlooker; but I always like to join in, wherever I am; I still do, even these days. You are put out because those French marauders smashed the place up and took everything away. When there's a war on that's what happens! . . . I threw the ruffians out. 'Clear off out of it!' I shouted – and they got the message alright, even if it wasn't French. Whereas you – you know how to parlez! Or didn't you want to have anything to do with common soldiers?

It isn't half cold in your house, Madame! High class coolth and high class pallor. But I go about in the sun, because I like to be warm, and I'm brown, like the women in Sicily. And when it rains my hair gets curly without the help of curling tongs: and I don't wear corsets either; everything as it comes, the way My Own One likes. I let my tongue run away with me sometimes – a touch of the verbal runs. That's all right by him – except he doesn't say runs, he says diarrhoea. But I don't have a sharp tongue any more than I have a pointed hooter: with me everything is rounded. Better to be rounded than wrinkled. And dimples! He's counted them. He counted twelve. I won't tell you where they all are!

I say, 'My Own One'; he's always referred to himself that way, even before, when us was just 'Mrs' Vulpius and son. I say 'us'

– does that bother you? My Own One was very dependent on me, and me on him. Is there anything finer than two people needing each other? You were his soulmate. Good! I'd never have begrudged him his soul, if only it had been a good soul! First you were his school marm, then I was. Only with me he learnt something different. You were seven years older than him, I was seventeen years younger. I could be your daughter, but I'd not have wanted to. You'd have taken me in tow and been very strict and made a proper court Miss of me. If that was ever possible.

In the long run it was easier for him to do without a noble soul. You get used to a nice warm bed. I was his warming pan. And as will happen: one year later I was brought to child-bed. 'Love created you: let love be granted you.' That was how he greeted his son. Our August! Our little lad! You really might have shared with us in our joy, you know. Johann Wolfgang von Goethe's own natural son! Because everyone knew all about it, and he never denied it either. And he really was like a father to your son Fritz – brought him up and educated him. And now you say all sorts of nasty things about our August: he's a drunkard, like his mother.

My Own One had lots of duties at Court and official posts and often had to go away: but he was always homesick for me and the little lad. He wrote us letters and brought back presents so I could doll myself up like the ladies in Weimar. Lengths of silk and bonnets. And if ever I got bored I used to go out. He didn't want me getting all gloomydoomy; and if I ever felt that I was getting that way I'd go out dancing or for a glass of wine, or skating and playing cards. When he came back I was just the way he wanted me to be: whizzy and sparky and full of the joys of spring. I am the way I am and he is the way he is. He wanted me like that and I wanted him like that. I was often really randy, like the girls in Italy. That means when you want to sleep with a man, Madame! Not just any man. *That* man! That can really give you the urge. And my urge give him a boost – every time: he wrote a new work, and I made something new, too.

But then nothing went right for me any more. It makes no odds if you know what I mean or not. I still howl over it to this day. Perhaps it just suits you down to the ground to have Frau Privy Councillor von Goethe crying her eyes out in Frau von Stein's house. That's a real laugh, that is! I'd sooner laugh than cry. They said at Court it was God's punishment, when one baby only lived a few days, and another one only drew breath for a few hours. And if your children are stillborn, well that's the inscrutable Will of God. You make of everything whatever you will.

The Carafe is still half-full. And I've still got a few things left to say, Madame.

His mother, the Frau Councillor in Frankfurt, called me 'her dear friend' and 'dear daughter' as well. She said I was his comrade-in-arms and that's exactly the right word – there was certainly a lot to take up arms about. And being driven about! With a coat of arms! On my very own carriage! That was a triumph, when he gave me the coach and I had the horses harnessed up and drove through the streets. That set the old lace curtains twitching all right! Meantime us lived in the hunter's lodge. 'Eroticum' he called it – but no one was supposed to hear that! Eros in Weimar! Are you going a bit red in the face, Madame? If our marriage-in-conscience was good enough for him, and if it was good enough for the Duke as well, then it certainly had to be good enough for me.

How much choice did I have? After all who would have taken me? Perhaps a chancellery clerk. Better to be the ladyfriend of a great man than the wife of a little one. And he looked after us like the most devoted of fathers. He took on my aunt, who brought me up from a little girl and my sister as well; and he went to a lot of trouble over my brother, as if it was his brother-in-law – got him a job at Court – and he wrote a will in favour of me and August, so that everything should go to us, if anything was to happen to him.

So why do you hate us then? I haven't taken anything away from you. What I gave to him was something you really didn't want to give – didn't have it *to* give, even. The way a person behaves when a thing's over, shows how much it was really worth in the first place. I know from the garden: nothing grows if you don't sow it.

Do you still remember the 14th October, 1806? Children learn that date now at school. The Battle of Jena! When the French soldiers laid waste the Frauenplan and swarmed into the house; and they were about to leap on My Own One, with their bare sabres. I threw myself between them and him. The men were completely plastered. I shoved a few candelabras in their arms and they pushed off. My Own One said he owed his life to me and from that day forth us belonged together more than ever before and now he was responsible for me. Three days later us got married.

*You* said: secretly; and only in the vestry, because Goethe felt embarrassed about the Vulpius woman. But that isn't true. The wounded were lying in the nave. That was why. The Top Minister of the church united us personally and afterwards I was an Excellency and our August could call himself 'von

Goethe'. And they started doing me the honours! I could *hear* the gnashing of teeth of the whole of Weimar when they had to receive the wife of Privy Councillor von Goethe.

And in spite of that I still went on having a game of cards, and going off to the theatre on my own – except in a box now! My Own One never put me under lock and key, and no more did I him. And now I'm going to ask you something: would the late dear departed Herr Oberstallmeister have married you again, after he'd had you for twenty years?

I love celebrating special occasions, and I love being any-where where people are having a good time, like if you're with actors. The people of Weimar can say what they like! When he was with you he wasn't allowed to wear his prophet's mantle *or* his carpet slippers either. You wanted to make a court poet out of him, with jabots and a wig and little embroidered weskits.

When he gets his catarrh and fever, then I make him a cold compress; and when he gets the shivers, then – it's off with the nightshirt! Not his! Mine, Madame, and I get him warm again. I am just as much up in meter and hexameters as you are; but he has tapped them out for me, on my bare back and on my behind. Long-short-short, long-short-short. They call that scansion. He calls my backside Callipygos. He saw the statue of Venus Callipygos in Naples – the Venus with the beautiful backside. After your time, Madame! How ever else was he supposed to get away from you? He *had* to run for it! Right across the Alps! Didn't anyone slip you a copy of his *Roman Elegies* to read? Secretly? Has his soul-mate stooped that low perhaps?

Why did you begrudge him his Roman Girls? I say he can have his little Minnas, and welcome. I call them all little Minna, whatever they happen to be called – Lily or Faustina or Charlotte. He lets me go dancing and I let him have his little Minnas. Just as long as he has someone that he can write his verses about. The girls think he's a nice old man.

He needs peace and quiet for his work. I racket about and make a lot of din, he says. He used to like it before, when us were in the gardenhouse. But now the house is full of people – young servants, boys and girls, and coachmen and a secretary and all the visitors who want to wait on him. There's always such a crush and a clamour, and that's why he goes off a lot. He once wrote to me that when he comes back: 'Night-time becomes the more beautiful half of life.'

You said that I was Goethe's 'fatter half' . . . Is that the kind of thing a noble soul should say? When I was little I often went hungry, and later on I had to swallow a lot, and a lot of that I had to wash down with something, or it would have come right back up again, and I'd have come out with it, right there in the inn, or on the street – what I'm saying now just to you alone. You've got a nice slim figure, Madame. And how long does it take your lady's maid to lace your bodice quite so tight? You certainly can't ever have enjoyed your meals much.

I love eating, and I love drinking – something really *good*, not cheap, sweet muck like this is. But I'm emptying the flask all the same! So that you won't have to alter your opinion and so, when you go round telling everyone that that Vulpius woman drank the decanter dry (and then had to go and pour out her heart to you), it won't be a word of a lie. I've got a lot of pains in my body, in my kidneys – perhaps a touch of gall bladder, too. It does me good to get it all off my chest every once in a way. You put it about that Goethe became all sensual because

of me – as if that was something bad, as if he's now no longer
the great Poet Prince of Weimar. I get pains, Madame: colic
pains and cramps. Pain makes some women thin, and some it
makes fat.

I am fifty. You are seven years older than My Own One, and
so you are now – it doesn't matter: we're both of us old women.
I wasn't beautiful. You have to beware of beautiful women – You
only ever find them in books or on the stage. I wasn't beautiful,
I was only ever pretty. For him I was a pretty girl with dark eyes
and curls and dimples. I always wore full skirts. I never laced
myself up. I didn't hold back. I was always generous. But apart
from My Own One, not one man came near me. On my honour!
I have my honour too, it's just a different sort. When I heard
that about the black pudding gone berserk, well that brought
my cramps on right away. People said that I had bitten Frau von
Arnim – Bettina. And all I had done was grab hold of her and
throw her out, because she was pestering him. Did the berserk
black pudding come from you as well? Our good Thuringian
black pudding!

So, Madame! The decanter is empty and I am full. I drink
on account of the pains, then it's all right for a while, and I
can show a cheerful face to the world. The sulphur springs in
Berka don't help, but a glass of punch helps all right – that's my
medicine.

It would have been quite all right for you to receive me,
Frau Oberstallmeisterin! When all is said and done I am
house-trained – I can be presented at court. I was allowed
to make my curtsey to the Duchess. The Duke asked me to
dance, and I took a turn round the floor with him, just the
same as with my other partners. If Mrs Schopenhauer can offer

the newly-spliced Christiane von Goethe a cup of tea then there's
no earthly reason why your port wine should be too good for her.
I'll have a case of our Samos sent round to you.

And now I'm off. I'm not quite steady on my feet any more. I'm
not putting any visiting card on your silver salver. I'm putting one
of My Own One's verses – addre. sed to me. Shall I read it out? Or
have you heard enough of the common Thuringian tones of that
Vulpius woman?

# No memorial for Gudrun Ensslin

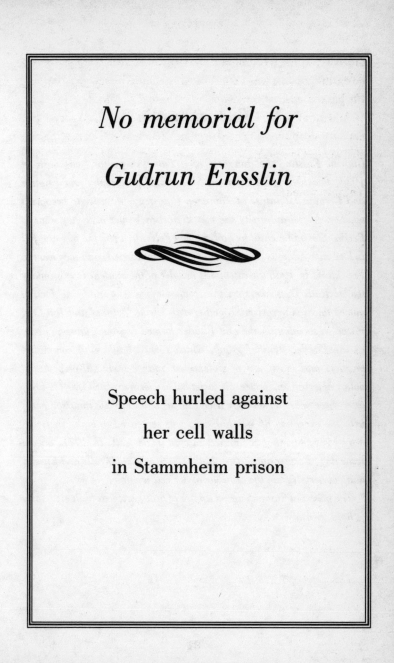

Speech hurled against

her cell walls

in Stammheim prison

# Gudrun Ensslin

*Gudrun Ensslin, the daughter of a Lutheran pastor, was born in 1934, fourth of seven children. She studied philosophy and English and German Literature at Tübingen University, in order to become a teacher. At the university she met Bernward Vesper and they went to Berlin. She had a child by him, named Felix. In 1967 she met and fell in love with Andreas Baader, whom she later married, and they went to Frankfurt. In 1968 the attempted murder of the student revolutionary leader Rudi Dutschke split the student movement, and one faction moved towards terrorism. Together with Ulrike Meinhof and Jan Carl Raspe, a sociologist, she and Baader formed a group, known chiefly as the Baader-Meinhof group, which robbed banks and committed murders and other acts of violence to finance their kill-or-be-killed policy of terrorising bourgeois society. They were arrested in 1972 and, after three years, eventually tried and sentenced to life imprisonment, with the exception of Meinhof, who was sentenced to eight years. In May 1976, Meinhof committed suicide in her cell. In 1977, on the same day, Baader and Raspe shot themselves in their cells and Ensslin hanged herself from the crossbar of her cell window.*

*The prison at Stammheim, a suburb of Stuttgart, was built especially to hold them.*

# No memorial for
# Gudrun Ensslin

Speech hurled against her cell walls
in Stammheim prison

I will talk when I want to talk and not when you want, you shit
faces! Even if I am only talking to the wall! Everyone only ever
talks to the wall! Why am I running about in my socks? Because I
can't stand hearing my own footsteps any more: tap-tap, tap-tap,
tap-tap. I prowl about like a cat, and then I pounce!

Pounce and pronounce!

Beasts of prey behind bars – untamed. We bite and we scratch
and we shit on you! The Big Cat Show from Stammheim, every
day, every evening on German television, on all three channels.
All that's missing is the tunnel for us to run in through. Why
don't you charge admission? They all get fat on us – the screws,
the judges, the journalists and the photographers. The public
most of all. We don't get any smell of a fee. For years now, every
single day, we've filled your newspapers for you. We bring in
more than we cost, Herr Springer! Twelve million DM to build

Stammheim prison. And what does the lead story on *das Bild* bring in? You shut us in, but you can't shut us up. So, we may not be able to smash skulls in any more, but we can still hit the headlines: 'The Federal Republic is controlled from within Stammheim!'

'The cushioned gait – long, supple step' –'. . . 'Long' is incorrect, Gudrun. Concentrate! Rainer Maria Rilke, 'The Panther.'

'It is, for him, as though there were a thousand bars, And through a thousand bars . . .' – Shit! You fat sows – I'm not talking to you. I'm not talking to anyone any more. Even the walls of the cell are a damn sight better than your ears. No talking, no eating, no more taking in, no more spewing out. Stop pissing and shitting. Finish! Total refusal. I wanted to hold back everything, and got cramps in my bladder. 'Gudrun, go to the toilet before you leave the house!'

I don't feel anything any more! I don't hear any voices any more. I line them all up: Father – Mother – Sister – Brother and give – them – the *chop*! Now when I stick a gramophone needle into my arm no blood comes out any more. I could join a circus and let them saw me in half.

To imprison imagination is murder! Imaginary – Solitary. So-li-ta-ry. You must order your thoughts, order the words, last words, 'les belles choses'. Damned Chose! I believe in the Revolution – well, you have to say *some*thing last. Whether anyone can hear it or not! 'Our Father in Heaven hears everything, my child!' Yes, Papa! You'll all have me on your fat consciences. You are to blame for my death. What you are doing is mass murder, the masses murdering the individual. But I'm still breathing for all that. I huff and I puff. Breathe in – breathe out – breathe your last. Five intakes of breath from wall to wall. It can be done in threes, and in two breaths.

My eyes are burning from the neon light, as if I'd been weeping. 'Even your tears are dry' – why can't I forget your stupid sayings, Vesper? I paint thick black lines on my eyelids here too. My face belongs to me. This is the only way you get me, the only way I come, like the aristocratic ladies at the guillotine. *The Last Woman on the Scaffold*, Gertrude von le Fort, classic example of a German novella. Compare Milly from Beckett's *Happy days* with *The Last Woman on the Scaffold*! First they make themselves up, and then they stick their hand grenades in their pockets. And – so? Whose grain does that go against – Mr Springer's? Doesn't our terrorist-look suit you? Do you want to stick us all in uniforms and ceremonial robes? The wardresses could break your heart: Stammheim for life – every day clock into the clink, clock out of the clink. You can strike the word compassion out of your vocab, Gudrun. You can't afford compassion. The first day I'd have liked to bite into the white flesh of your arms, but all I did was bare my teeth to put you on your guard. Winnie – she's called Winnie and not Millie! Winnie and Willie in the atomic dust; Adam and Eve at the end of time. My father-in-law: a major poet in the German language, Will Vesper! Will, not Willie!

'Holy Fatherland at hazard,
All your sons around you gathered –'

What do you think of the *daughters* of the Holy Fatherland, then, you Nazi pig! You have made the people daft and dull with your lyrics. The problem of happiness has never been an issue for me. You arseholes!

Yes, I suck away at my own arm, Mother, even though you

have forbidden it a hundred times. I make my own love-bites.
Nowadays, I'm a strictly non-relating person. I'm not the parson's daughter from Cannstatt any more, I am not my siblings'
sister any more; I was never married to the highly gifted writer
Bernward Vesper, I am not a teacher and I am not the mother of a
child! If you would only get that into your heads, once and for all!
It can't matter fuck-all to you, the nature of my relationship with
Andreas Baader. When I am dead – when I shall be dead – after I
shall have died – use the correct tense Gudrun! – you can mourn
for your lost child, and pray that God will have mercy on the dead
woman. Amen. 'One may turn away from earthly justice, but not
from the Grace of God.' Why can't I root Father's sayings out of
my head like a bunch of weeds? 'May the Lord be merciful unto
you and cause the light of His countenance to shine upon you.'
Neon light shines upon your daughter, Papa! I don't need your
Mercy. First it's words from the pulpit and then it's words from
the professorial chair – I shit on them! It's nothing to me any more
to say shit; but it doesn't give me any satisfaction either. Does
that satisfy you, Mother? When you produced that menagerie
of parson's children what expectations did you cherish?

But you were *always* cherishing expectations! Every one
of them a Child of God? But then how was I to protect my
child against the world? After all, how does one protect children? Wasn't it better, for my child and for all children to
come, to change the world? Conception, gestation, birth and
the whole process of breast-feeding were all important to my self-
discovery! 'Use fewer exclamation marks in your compositions,
Gudrun.' Child's name: Felix. Father's profession: freaked-out
intellectual, death by hanging. Mother's profession: terrorist,
murderess, arsonist; currently in Stammheim.

I don't react any more. 'Sticks and stones may break my bones but names can never hurt me.' I don't feel anything. Why doesn't my maternal instinct stir itself? I'm like a block of ice. I should be put in the deep-freeze, so that in a hundred years' time I can see — shall be able to see — what has become of our student movement. A date in history, a name, Saint Gudrun and Saint Ulrike and Saint Andreas — The Allsaints of Stammheim. Vesper with his Father-complex and me with my Father-complex and Felix with his Father-and-Mother-complex — it really is enough to turn your wits. 'There is only a thin line between madness and reason.' So I had politics on the brain, did I? What have you got against that? What have you got in your head? Slobbering all over the page, you literary bedwetter! You sired a child, but you weren't a father; and I carried a child and gave birth to it, but I was no mother. Your eternal: 'I must write!' Your shitty dialectic, off on a trip — setting out — arriving — starting-up — landing — dreaming — flipping — freaking out — freaking off! You freaked-out lump of horseshit. And for you I once lit black candles! What you needed was some little floozy. (*English accent*) 'I hate! I hate!' There wasn't anything else you could do, except hate: your father and your father land and the people, whom you called 'vegetables', because it sounded even more contemptible in English. Not loving anyone yourself, but wanting to be loved; and I, idiot, I fell right in. 'D'you love me? D'you love me forever and always?' Plus the inevitable, pitiful Fuck-and-make-up. A child got me with child and I plummeted onto the mummymill — and that turns and it turns! 'Gudrun — avoid sentences with an excess of assonance . . .'

Now I see everything, stone cold sober. The child had to be called Felix, so that the vegetables would notice what a happy child there was, growing up in a world which his parents had changed from the ground up, not one mingy step at a time. Which meant he had far worse luck with his parents than his parents did with their parents and *they* did with *theirs*. Couldn't you have looked after the child when the pigs nicked me? You're dealing with Intellectuals here, Mr High Court of Law – spare us the commentary! I couldn't take the child with me into prison, or on the run.

You see Papa, in my particular case it was the mother's life Herod was after, and not the child's! Why the hell do you all keep sending me those damned photos? I don't want to see another single one! This snivelling drivel: 'Do you recall our first summer? You must remember the park bench at Tübingen!' As if the River Neckar had something to do with it. You haven't understood a thing. Distributing a few pamphlets. That was all. Paper. You might just as well go fly a kite. There must surely be other ways of spreading enlightenment than paper and bombs. You have to take away from people – or destroy – what they care about: their power and their money – just get that into your skull! 'It is easier to destroy than to build.'

I don't want to let myself dwell on what's to become of the child. I have sacrificed my child to a grand idea. You could say, that I let the sentence stand. Student movement. A wave of politicising, out of which a storm has arisen that has seized hold of the entire western world. 'Listen, child, listen. Hear how the hurricanes blow.' I will not swim in your stream. I will not swim against your stream. I am a barrage in the stream of time! This irritating tendency towards high-flown rhetoric – I get that from you, Father. Whole sentences keep coming to me, ready-made. Grammar practice. A born schoolmistress: Give the female forms of Householder, Squatter, Politician, Capitalist. Feminist, Female Fanatic, Lady Terrorist. 'Account for the high proportion of women involved in terrorism.'

As if gender still mattered any more. We are sexless, hunted beings, always poised just over the trap, or already trapped, nothing in our heads but getaway plans and ways of spring- ing people. A scythe planted in the belly. 'Women won't let themselves be done to any more, but women can do absolutely everything.' Got it? We rebel like the men and throw bombs like men, we are more fearless than they are, we have nothing to lose. 'Policemen are pigs at whom it is legitimate to shoot.' Right on, Ulrike! That sentence made headlines! They fell on it like vultures, drooling! Vultures deserve to be shot, too. Once you get started there isn't anyone who doesn't deserve to be shot. 'Women's need to defend themselves has been bottled up for centuries.' Your capitalist order can only be upheld by force. Children are thrashed to death by their parents. Erroneous technical hypotheses are to blame for hundreds of thousands of people killed in traffic accidents. Social inequities are to blame for deaths from alcohol, and deaths from drugs and deaths from suicide. Because you cannot go on living like that – understand?

Why do you shout so much, prisoner-in-the-dock Ensslin? Why do you bellow your slogans out at the walls? Our bugs aren't hard of hearing.

I'll shout until I don't have a single tooth left in my head! We have thrown ourselves onto the wheels of history and got caught up in the spokes. Shit! What a stream of drivelling images and parables – like the daughter of a Swabian parson . . . The expressive young face of Gudrun Ensslin! All the bland smooth faces of the girls on the 'Wanted' posters. And? – Is there something? The Public Prosecutor, Counsel for the Prosecution, Counsel for the Defence – all men, setting out to hunt a few women. 'We women are martyrs in a great spiritual movement. The only way to overcome the fear of bombs, is to throw them yourself.' Not bad Gudrun! Apparently, in the air-raid shelter

I am supposed to have shouted out 'Bombs! Bombs!' all the time, with terrific enthusiasm. Three life sentences. Jointly; dastardly. What else? Something else? Murder and attempted murder, from the basest motives. You shits, you contemptible shits! We are not criminals. We go into politics for the same reasons that you make your wars, but we use other means. You can bring us to trial and you can condemn us, but you can't leave politics out of it. Our criminality is political and your politics are criminal. We were stronger than the police. The terrorists of today are the politicians of tomorrow. Politics are also at work in the law courts! Politics is everywhere, in bed and in kindergarten and at school. Everywhere there is oppression and torture and the exercise of force. Terror! 'Gudrun, translate the Latin *terrere* into German.' *Terrere* means: to frighten, to startle, to alarm; terrorise means to wield terror, to spread fear, to oppress, to rape the spirit.

But in fact all we did was take up the fight against the reign of profit. We only entered the lists after they passed that law. Once again: We are political prisoners! We are not criminals! Got it? I ask you, Mr Supreme Court of Law, how long is 'life' for someone who is hungry, whom you can put on a drip feed any time you like? What do you do, if I hang myself? Do you want to kill me three times over? Solitary confinement is torture! I decide the date of my death myself. You don't have any power over us. Force-feeding? First bloody well feed the people who want to eat! Millions of people are hungry. You want to use our trial to divert public attention from your nuclear missiles, which you can wipe out the lot with – everything – everything! And you reproach us for a few dead bodies! Your sums don't add up.

When we were allowed to listen to records in our cells and read books, why didn't you bring me Kafka's 'The Hunger Artist'?

Why is Kafka's 'The Hunger Artist' hungry? Essay subject for the Sixth Form. Day and night on the trapeze, quoted word for word. Why is Gudrun Ensslin hungry? She can't eat any more, she cannot manage to get her jaws open any more; she grinds her teeth and gnashes them. The children in Biafra are hungry from hunger. I hunger, you hunger, she, he, it hungers. 'We hunger and thirst after Your Righteousness.' The child was brought up with such high expectations of its own performance. In her parents' house well-known politicians were always coming and going. The public lose interest in a hunger artist after forty days and turn to other events. Or was it fourteen?

And now, what if they forget us? What if nobody comes to our wing any more? And even the vultures lose interest in us? We're only really dead when they stop talking about us – and not till then. How long will they remember who Gudrun Ensslin was? The Rosa Luxembourg of the seventies! When you've attained all your goals there's only one logical conclusion and that's suicide. When you haven't attained any of your goals there's only one logical conclusion and that's suicide. 'If two quantities are equal to a third quantity, then they are also equal to each other.' A principle of mathematics. The curriculum of life.

Go on – admit that you're afraid of us! That you want to annihilate us, burn us like witches! Allsaints of Stammheim, help me! 'The principles of dynamite – instead of the rules of grammar' – the life story of a schoolmistress, exclusive to *Der Stern*. So – how much do you pigs pay? Make a list of your teacher's favourite words: Now – quick – forwards – on the way – at once – change – spontaneous – today – radical. Which of you knows some more words?

'Death as the final beacon.' Gudrun Ensslin, the front page

story. The last tape from out of the death cell. Do you still need captions? Her last request was for mascara. Make up complete sentences with verbs and auxiliary verbs and exclamation marks! If you're talking you're not dead. I'm still alive! And nobody hears my words; nobody hears my footsteps. Sleep! Sleep the sleep of the just! But tomorrow morning your rest will be over and then it will be time for us three to have our rest. To shoot – to shoot dead. Construe the transitive and intransitive forms of to shoot.

Every condemned man has the right to a last wish. I could have divulged my last wish to that 'I-am-trying-so-hard-to-understand-you clergyman, but I couldn't get my teeth unclenched. When I see these people I get lockjaw. Such a terrible spasm! They should put the three of us in a common grave! Do you hear? You shitheads! Throw us into the pit together! We're never going to get out of here. This is the final trap. Now you have us. Bravo!

Cause of death: hanging. 'He hanged himself in the loft.' In the country that's how it's usually done. I'm a parson's daughter from the country. No barn and no rope; but the flex from the record-player and one of the crossbars at the window. It was agreed a long time ago. Your surveillance system doesn't work. Our Intelligence is way superior to yours. You cannot separate us. Only death can separate us. Or maybe not!

Once upon a time I really used to know what my idea was of a good life, and now what I imagine is somewhere to live that isn't a hideout, and monthly wage packets, not bank robberies. And the alarm clock rings and I get up and take a shower and dress Felix and make him his cocoa and take him to school – 'be careful how you cross the road' – and set grammar exercises, drink coffee in the staff room and talk about the programmes on television and about holidays on Sylt. We're saving up for a house in the country.

I feel terrible. It makes me puke! I make you puke! Solitary confinement becomes confinement of the imagination. No memorial for Gudrun Ensslin. Not a single line in the history book. An extract from history, the little Ploetz. 'There is only a thin line between madness and reason.'

I'm going barefoot, Mama! I have taken off the woollen socks you knitted so lovingly. I will cool my blisters on the cold concrete floor. I want earth under my feet, or grass, grass with the dew on.

*Only find out*

*the magic spell*

Effi Briest to old Rollo,

her deaf dog

# Effi Briest

*Effi Briest is the heroine of Theodor Fontane's novel of that name, which was published in 1895. Effi, the daughter of a country gentleman and his wife, is betrothed at seventeen to Geert von Innstetten, who was formerly a suitor of her mother's. After two months they are married. He is twice her age. Once a hussar, now an ambitious civil servant. They settle in a small dull town, where Innstetten is the local government official and there they lead a small dull life, which continues to be equally dull after Effi gives birth to a little girl. Then the arrival of a new commanding officer for the local regiment, Major von Crampas, introduces a little glamour. During Innstetten's absence on business in Berlin Effi succumbs to von Crampas' charm, but their affair is short and is all but forgotten when Innstetten is promoted to a new post and they move to Berlin. There, life goes on much more amusingly and pleasantly until Innstetten accidentally comes across letters from von Crampas to Effi hidden in her work-basket. Although the letters are six years old he feels duty bound to challenge von Crampas to a duel, and kills him. The Innstettens are divorced. Effi's parents refuse to receive her, though they send her some money. Finally, when they learn that she is ill, they relent and she goes back to them at their estate in Hohen-Cremmen and spends a winter and a summer with them before she dies of consumption.*

*Theodor Fontane was born in 1819 in Prussia and died in 1898. He was a pharmaceutical dispenser, a war correspondent and travel writer and secretary to the Prussian Royal Academy of Arts. He was fifty-six when he wrote the first of several novels, in which he often concerned himself with the predicament of women.*

# *Only find out*
# *the magic spell*

Effi Briest to old Rollo,

her deaf dog

That was the way Mother brought me up: every man is the right man. A good appearance, noble birth, good position. When I saw Innstetten for the first time I suddenly began to tremble all over. As if my body was trying to defend itself. But I didn't understand what my body was saying. I was always a little afraid, and in a way that was really what he wanted. I won't even mention about the ghost upstairs at Kessin. That was not right, and he was to blame for that, too. And if Crampas hadn't opened my eyes, then I would never have got over my terror. Innstetten wanted to use fear to bind me to the haunted house, to educate me and make me grow up. But he was a schoolmaster, not an educator. And someone who is still almost half a child, as I still was, should not be kept in constant terror.

Move up, Rollo! We'll sit here for a while on the garden bench.

Your eyes were always cast upwards, Innstetten. Bismarck only had to whistle and Innstetten was at his service. It was never like that at Hohen-Cremmen. Whatever else, my father always had something free about him, in everything he did, never any trace of the civil servant. He never wanted to set his sights any higher, so he was never afraid that he might fall, either.

I've always been full of yearnings – it's my nature. I had so much time for dreaming and soul-searching; and you were always so busy doing: you never yearned for anything. Your one goal was to achieve. The truth is, really, I was only just coming into bud; but you didn't understand anything about flowers, and not much about women either. You didn't help me to blossom. I am a blossom that's only half-opened, already withered. I was your precious little plaything, that's what you said yourself; and something like that – a plaything – it's something you get out for show; and you play with it and then you put it back in the drawer.

At home I never learned how to be on my own. Apart from my parents, here at Hohen-Cremmen I had my friends as well, and the garden and the swing, and the ornamental paths. At Kessin with you there were very few distractions, and what you called 'the quiet days'. And then the evenings, when you took the lamp and said, 'I still have work to do.' If you noticed that I was sad you would turn round, put the lamp on the grand piano and say, 'Play something, Effi!' And I would stand up obediently and play something, from *Lonengrin* or even from the *Valkyrie*. But Wagner was completely out of place at Hohen-Cremmen. Someone must have said, 'My dear Baron von Innstetten, Chopin is passé, Wagner's all the rage now!' You were thinking of your career and wanted to turn me into your helpmeet. It was what I wanted myself, to reach the highest heights – but more the way you do on a swing, not with all that bowing and scraping and being humble.

In the beginning I often used to tell you what I was thinking and feeling – it does mean *some*thing, after all, being a Briest! – but those sort of conversations used so easily to lead to ill-feeling. Once, when I said I had married you from ambition, you took it as a joke, and so it was too in a way; but in the end it does turn out to be the truth after all. But my ambition was for you and not for me. All women are like that.

And then – what you used to call 'little tendernesses'! I can see now the way you used to raise your hand up to ward me off. 'Really, Effi!' It always had to be dark, so that I shouldn't see your face, as if we were doing something forbidden. You determined when it was time for tendernesses; and if I stretched out my hand to you, ever, then you would give me a kiss on the back of my hand and put my hand back on top of my coverlet, and I would know my place – that's all for today, my dear Effi.

Actually your little tendernesses always frightened me – they always smacked rather of dominion, and of duty. You wanted to be not just the begetter of our little daughter Annie but a model husband and father. And so I had to go to the spa and take the waters. But it wasn't that. It was the way everything always had to go so strictly according to plan. I was for something a bit cosier; for the dunes. There has to be some passion to it, too: one should get a bit dizzy and the earth should move and it should be like on the swing – you fly up, and the rope suddenly yanks you back. Oh Innstetten! We should have talked to one another. Now I talk to Rollo instead. Whenever I used to say anything to you, you used to listen to me with great attention, and even agree with me; and all the same, in the end you still used to say, for the hundredth time: 'Best to keep everything as is'. That's the phrase that comes into my mind whenever I imagine myself talking with you. Lately I talk with you a lot, when I'm sitting here in Hohen-Cremmen by the sundial, with the dog lying beside me, growling in his dreams.

After the divorce, when Annie was allowed to visit me in Berlin for the first time in the Königgrätzerstrasse, what I really ought to have done was to run to you, just as I was. And not to the apartment – but to the Ministry! Not fallen on my knees in my room and prayed. It wasn't up to God, it was your doing. You had trained the child like a little parrot. 'Yes – if I'm allowed . . . .'. If I'm allowed?! You couldn't have had me shown the door, it would have created too much of a stir. You would have walked over to the window and turned your back to me. But you would have listened to me; and you would have put up your right hand yet again, and that would have meant: 'Really, Effi!'

My fear was greater than my anger. Anger makes you strong, fear makes you weak. I fell apart. Since then I have been getting weaker and weaker. Berlin wasn't big enough for the three of us. I didn't want to meet you by accident, and I didn't want to find myself standing on the pavement while you drove by in your coach with people saying there goes Minister Innstetten – for you will certainly be made a Minister soon. And I didn't want to lie in wait for Annie on her way to school, just so as to be able to see her. So then, when my parents finally took pity and fetched me back to Hohen-Cremmen, that was what saved me. When you married me you were twice as old as I was, and now you are still a man in the prime of life. And I am an old young woman. Later on the child will inherit the Briest family estate at Hohen-Cremmen. Or will you refuse to allow Annie to inherit from her cast-off mother? And it's true – what should she do with ornamental paths and a swing and a sundial? A lot of time has gone by.

I'm not accusing you, Innstetten, you are the way you are. But I am entitled to complain a little. You all loved me because I was the way I was; and now I'm not any more. And everyone was full of respect for you, because you are the way you are. So – in the end what is better? To be respected for a long time or loved for a short time? Father's answer to that would be to say what he always says: 'That is too big a subject!' I didn't know that there are some hedges and fences that you can't leap just like that. I never learned to steeplechase.

Now he's put his fat paw on my knee again. Are you trying to tell me it's time for our walk, Rollo? Everything should carry on as usual and keep to its appointed hour? The walking part gets just a little shorter each time, the pauses for catching our breath just a little longer.

Yes, Innstetten! Someone who has principles has the advantage – and I'll say no more on that subject. You have no love in you, and you can't help it and so perhaps you aren't really to blame after all. You said once that steadiness was not my strong point. You only ever said what I wasn't and what I didn't have. That's like the Ten Commandments. 'Thou shalt not.' But I need someone to tell me what I *should*! You fell in love with me when I was still half a child, because when you were young you loved my mother. The truth is, really, it was my mother you meant; and she would have suited you better. Father thinks so too. Everybody knew it, all except me. And what you wanted to do was to finish off educating the other half of the half-child to suit yourself.

And now, finally, we have to talk about Crampas too, Innstetten! You see, Innstetten, Crampas let me be, just as I was; he didn't want anything, and I didn't want anything too. Suddenly you are flying and the ground falls away from under your feet, you think at any moment the rope is going to snap and then it doesn't at all, you're back on your feet; but afterwards you're not ever the same again. In Kessin, they said about Crampas that he was a ladies' man. He took women seriously; or at least he took them just as seriously as he took his commission – or the whole world, for that matter. He didn't take anything completely seriously. And I did say 'No'! I resisted him, and he pressed his attack. And it went on like that, back and forth. But I liked it, him pleading with me and being so urgent.

Our horses kept so close together, they flew along, side by side. Once, we were galloping and he shouted across to me: 'Opportunity is the Mother of Love.' First we put the horses to a trot and then we just gave them their heads – yes that's probably the way *you* would express it. Crampas didn't always put things very delicately. And I think that there was something in me too that was – I won't call it common – something sensual.

Being unfaithful made me into a woman, not being married and having children. We simply got carried away, that's all. There's a Something inside me. I couldn't talk about it to anyone. It wasn't really up to adultery. Jesus and the Woman taken in Adultery! Father has a book with engravings, and there the adulteress is lying at the feet of our Lord and he is stretching out his hand to her, to raise her up out of the dust. I took another look at the picture, but it isn't about me. Perhaps because everything looks so different from the dunes, almost oriental somehow.

Yes, the dunes and the sea, sometimes I long for them. I felt better there than anywhere else in the world. No one could see you and you couldn't see very much, but you still did have views, and the booming sound. It was like a game of hide-and-seek with the wind; it would snatch you up and then let you go again.

Everyone has a landscape that they belong to. For me it was the dunes: blind, hidden; and that isn't good. Father belongs in the open fields, cross-country, where he can disappear behind the next bluff. And you suit Berlin best, with the straight streets and broad staircases that lead up to the Ministry. And Mother – where does she fit in? She never got to where she would have belonged, either. It's hard to find out what is right for you; and then it's even harder to get there and stay there.

I am dreaming my day-dreams again. That trip that time, on New Year's Eve, going over the ice; it was very dangerous; and I was sitting with Crampas in the same sleigh; and you were in the other one; and you said afterwards that you had had the sensation that I had gone under with Crampas; and you had been afraid. Oh if only I had! Crampas liked living, but he could have left off just as easily. There was nothing he set very great store by – he had no wish to own anything. He pulled me to him; and then he would let me go again.

I should have drowned myself. All unfaithful wives must drown themselves. And there was certainly enough water there. But there was the child. And if the Governor's wife had drowned herself, everything would have come out and in the end I would still only have destroyed your career. Just to keep on going like that, gently, first of all through the shallows, then on into the waves, until your feet don't touch the bottom anymore, it can't be all that bad, surely; and Crampas would certainly have come with – there was something about him; you could have gone under with him. He wasn't cut out for living. Now I don't have anyone left. No one to live with and no one to die with. All I have now really is Rollo. Ssssh, Rollo! Quiet, that's a good boy. Lie still. The sun will keep us warm for a little while yet.

But in the end the current wasn't quite strong enough after

all, otherwise I wouldn't be sitting here at Hohen-Cremmen, back with my old parents, making problems for them. 'Zephyr's daughter', Mother once called me – that's a long time ago. She said I had a touch of the circus rider about me. She talked about trapeze artists too. You both looked at me, as if you wanted to say: 'Really, Effi!' But for all that, you both had a taste for things that were not quite proper.

Innstetten has his age and I have my youth, I thought; and I even used that against you – after all there had to be one trump in my hand for me to take the trick with. You provided everything that reason dictated. You couldn't do anything about your age any more than I could about my youth; but everybody acted as if my being so young and already the wife of a governor and the mother of a child was somehow to my credit.

All our sins must be paid for on this earth. That's the sort of thing you're fond of saying. The older I get the less I believe in sayings. The Sun puts the day to bed! It wasn't the sun; a lot of things had to come together, pure chance – the sort of thing people call chance. But nothing happens by chance. I should have talked to you – before we set off from Kessin to go to Berlin. But when I said how frightened I had been in the haunted house and tried to tell you all about my fears, you immediately put on your schoolmaster face. And really the whole business with Crampas was already behind me.

You can only confess something when you have a hope of being forgiven. But no one was ever meant to understand it. Why didn't I burn his letters? Sometimes I saw them, at the back of my sewing basket; I picked them up in my hand, but even then I didn't ever read them. I just wanted to remember: Effi, that's the sort of woman you are! Not in the way you look back at something beautiful; but at something wicked. But you shouldn't ever forget those things either, and I would always think: it wasn't only wicked, it was beautiful too.

When I told the first lie I thought the roof was going to fall in; but it didn't. The second one already came much more easily. The fact is that everyone wants to believe what you say; and really there isn't anyone at all wants to know the truth if they can help it.

You suspected something, Innstetten. Do you know what I sometimes think, when I sit here parading my life before me in my mind's eye, and the shadows on the sundial keep reminding me that everything passes? Even without Crampas and the dunes it wouldn't have got any better. That's something I've come to understand now, too. Lightweight! Really, yes, that was what I wanted – I wanted everything to be light and easy. To be Baroness Innstetten for the rest of my life, and one day perhaps the wife of the Minister, with state balls and invitations and four weeks at a spa every year – well! with that prospect even the things that are supposed to be diverting become boring. You had your career and I had my boredom. And when you got back from being important I was supposed to rush headlong to greet you and admire you. But that was something Rollo could do just as well. Quiet Rollo! Good dog! Go back to sleep. We'll have our walk in a little while. It will be dusk quite soon and another day will be over.

I've thought about things a lot, Innstetten! The penalty for love is death; and for murder – because murder was what it was, even if you called it a duel and a matter of honour – for murder you get six weeks and get pardoned, and after a short time your career goes on as before. But the truth is, I was the one who was guilty. The guilty party ought to have been summoned and given a hearing. As if it all had nothing to do with me! I just had to be sent away somewhere out of the way. Banishment for life, that was the sentence you gave me. Dismissed like a servant who had stolen a few silver spoons. If you had only stood by me! And we would have emigrated to America – lots of people do start their lives all over again there. Or if we had even come back to Hohen-Cremmen together! Farming is something that you can learn, and Father's getting old. Surely even you are not so absolutely indispensable in your post, Innstetten.

And what now? Just to keep on going, with Honour and Duty – the truth is, that's not so wonderful either. Odd bits of news filter through to us here and reach my ears, even though everyone tries to keep things from me. In the beginning I thought: Innstetten's honour will soon be restored. For a while people will go on saying: 'Poor Innstetten!' And perhaps someone might even say: 'His poor wife', and: 'after all she was still so young'. But the time would come when you would look for a new wife, perhaps even a wife who looked a little like your Effi, but who had a bit more steadiness, and who didn't need any more educating; and who would be a better mother for the child. But if none of it turns out well, Innstetten . . . well *that's* what I mean: Crampas dead, you with your duty, the child being a good girl at school, and me here with poor old Rollo, fast asleep while I talk away, who only lifts his head when I mention his name . . . Yes Rollo, good dog. Go back to sleep.

When you sacked me, just like that, and I couldn't go back to Hohen-Cremmen, and at one fell stroke a divorced Briest became a divorced Innstetten, and the days in the Königgrätzerstrasse drifted by doing needlework and playing Patience and Chopin! And no one said: 'Play me something on the piano, Effi!' I would even have played something from the *Valkyrie*! And there was only ever Roswitha to drink tea with,

with her grisly stories. If I had had some work that I could do, if I had ever learned anything . . . But a divorced Baroness was not supposed to earn her own living, and my parents provided for me as best they could. It certainly wasn't what I'd call a real Fate. At Bad Ems the name of Anna Karenina was bandied about, but none of those ladies had really read the novel, it was all tittle tattle. And I had only had a tiny nibble at Fate. When I examine myself it's not so much guilt that I feel as shame, the way a child feels ashamed because it's done something forbidden and got caught. And I suppose you punished me, really, just as you would punish a child. Go and stand in the corner! Keep quiet!

Roswitha – she had her fate. When her illegitimate baby died and her father went for her with a crow-bar and she didn't know where to turn . . . That's when she wanted to drown herself and that's how she was when I found her. She has always had to work for her living, but at least with me she struck quite lucky. Compared with hers, my fate is a bit skimpy. Real destitution – I suppose that might have made me grow up and mature; but just to be abandoned, and with so much time all the time, and no one who needed me – even my parents would have a much more peaceful life without me . . . It isn't easy to be the parents of someone like Effi Briest.

You pronounced your sentence on me. But you are not God the Father. You are Baron Innstetten. I have always been less frightened of God than of you. And then I think: Everything happens over and over again. Springtime at the zoo. Whether it's fifty visits to 'Unter den Linden' or five hundred. And every few years a new fur muff to keep me in a good mood.

I really did have it once, that sparkle; and my skirts used to rustle when I walked and people would whisper: 'What a handsome couple!' I went from being one in a hundred to being one in thousands, because I have this confusion inside me, and this darkness. Yes I did have a dark side to me, too, and none of you had the slightest inkling. Perhaps Gieshübler did, in Kessin, and Privy councillor Rummschüttel in Berlin; but even they could only offer me a powder to take, to calm me down.

Everything comes to pass so quickly and then it passes by and fades away out of sight. It's only a minute ago that I was sitting here on the swing, and then I was by the cradle in Kessin, and now I'm sitting here again looking at the swing. Nature arranged things very badly: a mother already at seventeen. But you can't go against Nature. My body could conceive a child and carry it, but my soul wasn't ready for it yet.

Sometimes I think, when yet another summer has gone by: I'm just like a leaf that the August wind has torn off too soon; and the leaf has dropped into the stream and been swirled away. First into a river, then into a torrent, and now I'm drifting toward the open sea. But these aren't your sort of ideas, Innstetten, notions about leaves blowing in the breeze and souls adrift with the tide. But all the same I did stay afloat – I didn't go under; and I'm actually a bit proud about that now. And the sea and the sky and whether we get through or go under, in the end it's all one and it's all up to God.

I feel totally at peace now, Innstetten. It will be better for you when you aren't a divorced man any longer but can say: 'My wife is dead.' Then perhaps you may be able to bring yourself to speak my name again and perhaps even, later, think: 'My beloved Effi'. Mother will come out soon with the rug and say: 'Really, Effi – you'll catch a chill!' and she'll put my shawl round my shoulders; she won't give me a hug, and I won't hug her, just say thank you, and smile and hold her hand for a second.

'Men who are men and women who are women' – another truly Briest saying. But then on top of that there are daughters! I'm still the same Effi Briest from Hohen-Cremmen. You all used to look on me with such admiration, but it was nothing to do with me at all. Being young and pretty and having a kind of natural charm doesn't really amount to much and I hadn't actually done anything. I had a baby. Every woman can do that, and in any case, really it was nursed and brought up by Johanna, and later by Roswitha. I have only ever played supporting roles, I have never been given the lead. A divorced Baroness von Innstetten and a divorced Briest.

So now I stroke Rollo's fur that's all grey now and getting a bit mangy too, and sometimes I stroke the silk that covers my thighs. Actually I do have a rather affectionate nature. Mother's temperament is much cooler and Father keeps everything at arm's length, even me. He'll let handfuls of corn trickle through his fingers, or he'll give the horses a great slap on the rump. Sometimes when I was little he would catch hold of my hair and ruffle it, exactly the way he would with his pointers if they dropped a partridge at his feet; and then I would lay my doll down at his feet, like them. And when Mother used to pull my bow straight and warn me not to be so wild – well, that was her way of showing affection. Why didn't I bath my baby and change its nappies with my own hands? The maids knew how to do everything far better than I did; and I always thought something might happen to the baby if I hugged her to me and kissed her the way I did with my dolls. And later on I used to pull her bow straight too.

We all live so far away from each other. The distances between us are too big. Gieshübler tried to bridge them, with a nosegay, or a little note at the right moment. If I had gone to him in the

pharmacy, no one could ever have said anything — there couldn't
be anything to fear from someone who was practically a cripple.
He liked me and I liked him too. If only I had *said* that I had to talk
to somebody, not just chit-chat; and he had seen how desperate I
was . . . But then he would only have been embarrassed and just
fetched me yet another of his powders. He guessed a lot. Once
he sent me a little book. Inside was written: 'For the romantic
Effi von Innstetten: Yet another Admirer'. Poems by Eichendorff.
Crampas used to quote verses by Heinrich Heine and you never
knew whether you should laugh or look the other way. I often used
to sit there with the book on my lap and read a few lines and then a
word would suddenly hit me, and I would forget the book and just
sit there and dream. I stopped reading the poems around then; but
lately I got them out again and I found a pen mark in the margin
of one page, and now I read these lines over and over and mutter
them to myself all the time:

> Each thing on earth contains a song
> That lies there, dreaming on and on:
> If only you find the magic spell —
> The whole world will rise and sing as well!

I haven't found my magic spell yet, Innstetten. No one can come
to you with a magic spell, you immediately lift up your hand to
ward it off. 'Really, Effi, must you . . . ?' When I try very hard
just to listen quietly to my inmost self, that's all I can hear:
'Really, Effi!' Sometimes it sounds amused, sometimes cross.
That was never a magic spell, that was a spell that destroyed
any kind of magic. I can imagine that when I am dead that's what
they'll write on my tomb: 'Really, Effi!'

Because that isn't right either, me dying so young. It will seem
like a reproach.

# *Desdemona – if you had only spoken!*

The last quarter-of-an-hour
in the bed-chamber of
Fieldmarshal Othello

# Desdemona

*Desdemona, in Shakespeare's tragedy* Othello, *is the daughter of Brabantio, a senator of Venice. She falls in love with Othello the Moor, a high-ranking army officer and hero of the wars; flouting convention and her father's wishes, they marry. Othello is sent to command the army at Cyprus and Desdemona goes with him. They are accompanied by Desdemona's maid Emilia and her husband Iago, one of Othello's officers. Iago is secretly consumed with resentment at having been passed over for promotion, and with jealousy of Othello, whom he suspects of having slept with Emilia. Iago persuades Emilia to steal an embroidered handkerchief, a sentimental treasure that Othello has given to Desdemona. Through devious intrigues Iago then uses the handkerchief to convince Othello that Desdemona has been unfaithful to him with another officer, Cassio. In the play* Othello, *heartbroken at this news, strangles Desdemona and discovers too late that it was not she who deceived him, but Iago.*

# *Desdemona – if you had only spoken!*

The last quarter-of-an-hour in the
bedchamber of Fieldmarshal Othello

'Peace and be still!' you said.

No, Othello, no! I will not hold my peace. There are things I
have to discuss with you, right here in our bedchamber. Do you
want to turn our bed of love into a battleground? Does everything
have to end in blood? You are a Fieldmarshal. Do you want to
turn murderer, now? Put up your dagger, Othello! Don't touch
me! Is that to be your last act of heroism? Killing the wife who
loves you and who was faithful to you from the very first breath
to the very last? A wife who is making no attempt to defend
herself? You can still kill me in a quarter-of-an hour's time. I
will have this quarter-of-an-hour. Once, I put my whole life in
your hands, Othello; don't be stingy – give me fifteen minutes
as a present.

You have just struck the cheeks that you used so often to
cover with kisses. You have struck a Venetian lady in the face.

Who are you, who dare to do such a thing? Are hands all you have? Do you think and feel only with your hands? Now you are making them into fists. Are these the same hands that used to encircle my neck so tenderly? I implore you, Othello, send that strength of yours back again into your heart and into your head. Nothing can be achieved with fists, not even if you're a commander-in-chief.

Is there after all so little understanding lodged in that great, beautiful head? In that great big beautiful body, such a tiny heart? You put your trust in a scrap of stuff that is used for blowing one's nose, or mopping one's brow, or even to wipe away tears. Do I have a rag-merchant for a husband, a weaver of linen? Your father gave the little napkin to your mother. And you gave it to me as a bridal gift – you did not have very much that you could give. I was spoilt, Othello. But I took care of the napkin and brought it with me to Cyprus. Ought I to have looked after it more carefully? Could I have foreseen that someone would spirit it away from me? That I would be surrounded by thieves in your house? Ought I to have known that you would turn this love-token against me? I was gullible, Othello, I was only too trusting. It never crossed my mind that a little piece of stuff would suffice to prove me guilty of being unfaithful. Me! Desdemona!

If I were guilty, my death would do nothing to appease your jealousy; but if I am innocent, all the guilt falls on you – you will not be able to go on living, or even want to. Ah, if only my father had laid me in chains, if only he had locked me behind iron bars! Except that I would have burst the chains, and bent the bars with my bare hands, to follow the man I loved. I was dazzled by the whiteness of your eyes. Your skin was as brown as mace. No one I had ever seen before was like you. Beside you, all Venetians became pale and sickly.

When you recounted to me – for the first time! – your great, heroic deeds, I sighed and even cried. I admired you and was sorry for you and envied you. My heart was filled with pity, but with envy, too. In those days I wanted to be a man and wreak havoc amidst all Venice's enemies. But of course I was only a well-bred young girl of good family, endowed with beauty and a gentle spirit. You were a stranger; you seemed to be a hero. Have I not given you sufficient proofs of my love? If you insist that Desdemona has been unfaithful, then you are insulting the man she loves. Do you believe that your place could be taken by a man like Cassio? Do you not know your own worth, Othello? Haven't my vows to you made you even more precious? Could you not say to yourself every morning: 'Desdemona loves me! Desdemona reveres me! The daughter of Brabantio, of a Venetian Senator!' Haven't I confessed my love for you quite openly – before the Prince of the Venetian State? Haven't I journeyed with you to this far-off land, far from Venice, far from the companions of my childhood, far from my father, who is so angry with me? Or do you want to make my father's curse come true: 'She has deceived her father, and may thee'?

No – don't say anything just now! Hear me out!

Should I have held you tighter, said to you afresh each evening: 'It is you that Desdemona loves; she loves your dusky skin, which is as brown as the wet sand on the Cyprus sea-shore'? Should I have whispered in your ear, the way the courtesans do? I was never taught how to speak of my feelings. A woman should keep herself in check and be reticent. How silly that is! And how deadly the consequences! Should I have sung the praises of your great exploits over again every day, recited the names of every battle? I chose a strong man and now you are so weak, Othello. My heart is filled with pity. I don't envy you any more.

You are spreading your fingers. Don't you want my pity? Stay where you are! Not another step! Do you want to throttle me? I won't cry for help. But I will talk louder, because you seem to be deaf. Everyone may hear what I have to say to you. Or do you only pay attention to things that people whisper in your ear? Why don't you just ask openly? You don't talk *about* someone, you talk *with* them! Instead of talking with your adversary – and now I am your adversary! – you reach for your weapon. Someone has only to whisper to you on the stairs, or in an alleyway, and you believe him. Go ask my waiting-woman for goodness' sake, whether perhaps she slipped my hankie to Cassio. She is Iago's wife, after all. Has this Cassio ever so much as mentioned my name, even once? In an improper way? Think about it, Othello; there are still ten minutes – scour your memory. And scour your heart. Perhaps all this is simply the work of Iago, who is jealous of your power and your good fortune. He was up to no good from the very beginning. Do you have no insight into people at all? Are you some sort of Holy Fool? Iago has turned that good man Cassio (yes! he is good, and utterly devoted to you, and his sweetheart is a girl called Bianca – everybody here knows that – except you. Why didn't you ask him, man to man?) – Iago has turned him into a drunkard. Iago is quicker than you, and he's cleverer, if cunning can be called cleverness. He hates you, and he hates Cassio, who you have given promotion to. I didn't know that he hated me, too. He sees people's weaknesses and he exploits them. Cassio's weakness was wine; yours is jealousy.

Yes, Othello, jealousy is a weakness. And my weakness

was that I took our love for granted. Othello and Desdemona – the great love story! How arrogant of me! What vanity! White Desdemona and her black Othello. I was conceited; I prided myself on having transcended every barrier and all the seas between us by bestowing my love on this stranger. The renowned Commander-in-chief, Othello, is to be sent overseas to Cyprus, by the Prince of Venice, to protect the island and the State of Venice from the Turks; and brave little Desdemona requests permission to travel with him, like a Courtesan. Yes, there was a touch of vanity, too, I admit it, it wasn't only love. And therein lies my fault. And now we've come to the point where our love-without-end has got to prove itself. The question I ask you is this: do you want to go down in history as a murderer? Do you know what awaits you? The Prince will recall you to Venice and arraign you before a tribunal – unless my father's henchmen avenge me first.

If you are deaf, Othello, if you don't understand my words and the language of my eyes any more, then do you still understand the language of my hands? Let my fingers speak to your fingers, my lips to your lips. If you don't believe in words any longer, believe the truth that lies in my gaze, in my hands, my shoulders.

They say that the one who loves more suffers more, too. Then was my love for you still not enough? And does that carry the death penalty? Who is to be judge? Who are you, that you may judge? You asked whether I have said my bedtime prayers yet. Yes, Othello, I have said the Lord's prayer, as I do every evening. How often I have just reeled it off without thinking and never guessed that one day I should need help so terribly. Othello would protect me from every danger – that was my great comfort. My earthly father had cast me off because of you. You don't know our Christian prayers. I have lived in my world and you in yours. Neither of us has really let the other in; neither of us has tapped on the other's door. But every evening I prayed: 'Take care of Othello!' It sounded as if I was giving my God orders. I ought to have prayed with you: 'Watch over both of us!' I ought to have taught you our prayers. Our prayers go: 'Lord, Thy Will be done!' Then can it be God's Will that the man who loves me above all things, should kill me? For me you were larger than life, greater than any other human being. I placed you on a pedestal and made you a hero, a god.

That angry redness has gone from your face, Othello; you have turned pale under your dark skin. You, too, are a man like other men. You can be wounded, and I am crying, because I am to blame that now you are standing before me a wounded man. But don't diminish yourself still further! I see your eyes shining, too. My time is up, Othello. Lay your heavy hands around my neck for the last time.

And now I don't have a handkerchief to dry my tears – lend me yours; you have so often. Don't you have a pocket handkerchief in your jacket? How is that, Othello? Haven't I hemmed dozens of hankies for you, and embroidered them beautifully, too? I chose silk, sometimes linen – I always had so much time to think about you, when you were away. Where have all those little handkerchiefs got to, then? They were pledges of my love. Tell me! Where did you lose them? Who did you give them to?

Ssh, sshh! Be still. Ssh . . . calm yourself, there'll be plenty of time for you to look in all your pockets. The pockets of your trousers, Othello, look there, look there! Perhaps – it is possible – perhaps you used it to wave to someone with? Or perhaps you had to dry the tears from someone's tender cheeks and left the hankie there. Such tiny bits of cloth are so quickly mislaid. Should I help you look? Hold still! Let me get to the inside pocket of your jacket. You are still ticklish then, Othello? How mightily your heart is beating, and how warm you are! There are drops trickling down your chest. Your whole body is weeping. Do you remember our first evening in Venice? When I unbuttoned your doublet and you weren't wearing any shirt underneath, and I saw your great black body, and I took fright – I had never seen a man's naked chest before – and I just had to laugh aloud for joy that all that belonged to me and then we . . . Othello – do you remember? I blush just to think of how I . . . how you . . . we . . . Othello, you are naked this time, too, under your doublet!

And now we neither of us can help laughing!

Othello!

# *Where did you lose your tongue, Mary?*

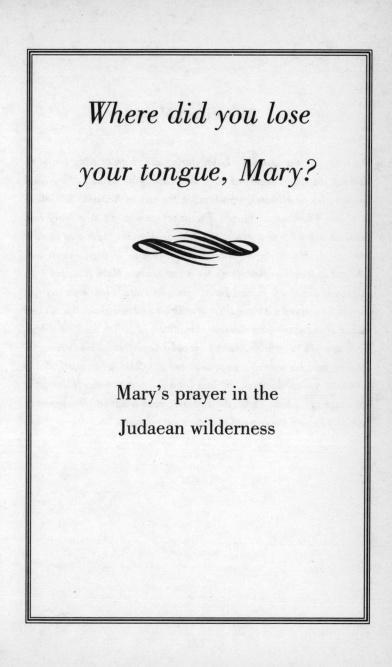

Mary's prayer in the
Judaean wilderness

# The Virgin Mary

*According to the Gospel of Luke, during the reign of King Herod in Judaea an angel appeared to a certain virgin, named Mary (and known also as Miriam), who lived in the city of Nazareth in Galilee and was betrothed to Joseph. The angel announced that Mary had been chosen to bear the son of God, the Messiah, who was to save the world. Shortly before the baby was due to be born Joseph was obliged to travel to Bethlehem for a tax census; Mary travelled with him, and the child, named Jesus, was born there. From an early age he was concerned with questions of religion and morality, and studied at the synagogue in the dialectical tradition of Jewish rabbinical law, finding much to question. As he grew older he performed many miracles and he and his teaching soon acquired a following, in particular a group of young disciples. He was tried for heresy before Pilate, the governor of Judaea under the Romans, and crucified. His teaching initially formed the basis of the Christian religion.*

# *Where did you lose
your tongue, Mary?*

Mary's prayer in the
Judaean wilderness

Our Father, which art in Heaven! Your son, who was my son, too, remained alone in the wilderness for forty days and nights. I won't be able to stay for so long. I am old. I want to speak with You. Perhaps You will send your angel to me once more, so that I can understand what I can't understand. I have broken Your commandment. I ought not to have left Jerusalem. We are supposed to honour the Sabbath and keep it holy. But I must speak with You, Lord. Where else could I do that? I am at my wit's end. I passed through the gate unnoticed – the streets seemed to be empty; the men were in the temple and the women in their houses.

Listen to me, Lord, I implore You! Today, my God, I am not speaking from among the chorus of the disciples, I am speaking to You alone. Forgive me if I say 'my God' and not 'our Father', as your son taught us to.

125

He said that you must forsake father and mother and brothers and sisters, and even yourself, if you want to follow Him. Why are we supposed to forsake the very people it is easiest for us to love? Are we meant to divide our love, and subdivide it, so that there will be enough of it to go round for the ones that no one loves?

One of them says to another: 'Jesus says . . .', they say; they don't say 'He *said*'; because for us he is always here among us. Of John, they say, 'The disciple that Jesus loved.' Even *He* loved one more, and the others less! And I love John as a mother loves her son, although he is not of my flesh. When he was hanging on the cross, Jesus's eyes rested on me for a moment, and He knew me. And He knew John, and said to him: 'Behold, this is your Mother!' To me He said: 'Woman, behold, here is your son!' He didn't say 'Mother' to me. By then I had already stopped thinking: 'my son'. I thought of Him as your son. He had already addressed me as 'woman' once before, in Cana, where they were to celebrate this wedding. I said to Jesus – He was there too – : 'They don't have enough wine for everyone!' He waved me away. He said: 'Woman, what have I to do with you?'; and He said His hour was not yet come, and I didn't know what He meant by 'His hour'. But the first miracle He did in my presence! Is it too much for me to think, Lord, that it was done for my sake, too? So that I would know that He was that other, quite different one, the one I had nothing to do with? Was that how it was?

Where are You, God? They say that You sit on a throne, always in motion, the way everything is in motion – the sun, the moon, the stars, the shadow which circles around me? Or are You the still centre? Does everything circle around You? Does Jesus really sit at your right hand? Who sits at your left?

Are You going to send a son again to deliver us? And then will that one sit at Your left hand? A lot of people now are having themselves buried in the Vale of Kidron. On the day of judgement, when the graves open, they want to be close to the spot where the angel rolled the stone away from the grave. A lot of people have little stones put in front of their grave, as if they didn't have confidence in the strength of an angel. They say, 'He will sit in judgement over us', and they are overcome with fear. They are afraid of Your judgement! They fight against fear by praying and singing. Father in Heaven! Our life is not easy. We are afraid on Earth. Do we have to be afraid of Heaven too?

After His death the disciples of the Lord took me into their midst. I closed up my house and left the key in the door and went off with them. Was that your will? We pray for 'Our daily Bread'. I have learnt to say 'our', where I used to say 'my' before. I asked the disciples to call me Miriam again, the way I was called as a girl. They forgot very quickly that I used to be that Mary, that bore the Son of God. The Son of God, who is with You now and sits at Your right hand, from whence He came, where He belonged, and from whence He will come again. Miriam. That means the one who is contrary. You know very well how contrary I was! I wanted to be like other women! No one asked me if I wanted to be chosen! Joseph regarded me with awe, and often with fear! He wasn't asked either. My angel called me 'highly favoured' and 'blessed'. He said: 'Fear not.' But I was full of fear. I didn't just marvel, the way you marvel at a miracle. I asked my angel, and He answered me. He said that Elisabeth, my friend, who was already old, would give birth as well – with God there is nothing that is impossible. I trusted her as I would trust a mother. I went to her across the mountains, and we looked at each other and put our arms around each other, and told each

127

other what we knew. We confided our secrets to one another. We stayed together for many weeks. Wherever we went flowers burst into bloom – hibiscus, jasmine, roses, poppies. We trod on carpets of blossom, and fruits ripened at our touch. We had only to reach into the branches to find our hands filled with pomegranates, blue figs! Our bodies were blessed. Let me speak of it once again, Lord! For who else is there for me to speak of it with? *Then* I didn't need any angel. But later, after the birth, I was just an empty husk, that has had the fruit taken out, and it dries right up.

Was it wrong of us to keep an eye on Him when we took Him with us to Jerusalem for the first time, to the temple? He was only a child after all – twelve years old! Two whole days we hunted for Him! When we finally found Him, in the temple among the scribes, I scolded Him, the way you do – a disobedient boy; and He put me in my place with one single sentence, as if it ill behove me to speak to Him in the temple; to Him – the son of God. And He didn't speak at all the way a son ought to speak to his mother. From that moment on I held my peace, but I stored up His words in my heart and thought about them, and did my work and was a woman amongst other women in Nazareth, who runs her house, does the washing, cooks the meals . . . At the well they would tell me all kinds of miracles that this Jesus had wrought, marvelling at it all, but not believing it. I said nothing, and I didn't marvel, because I did believe it.

But it's hard, Lord, to believe that a child that you yourself have brought into the world, that you've given the breast to and rocked to sleep, that that child is supposed to be at one and the same time a child of man, and the Son of God. Who was I to ask? Who knew any more than I did? The priests and the scribes? Or Joseph? The angel has never appeared to him again either. At night, when I got up and went to kneel in our little courtyard under the fig tree, and called out to my angel, Joseph came and said; 'Who are you talking to?' But I didn't answer him. I just followed him into the house. My angel only appeared to me as long as I was carrying Your son. But I saw him with my own eyes, I heard him with these ears. The angel only appeared to Joseph in a dream. Joseph! He often used to read the Holy Scriptures. His lips would move as he read, and I read from his lips what You had foretold to us through the prophets. Women listen, they don't read. And they don't talk as much as men, either, they've always got something that needs doing. But You gave us a tongue and lips as well, for forming words; inside our heads there are thoughts trying to get out. I am almost suffocated with this silence that You have laid upon me!

Our Father which art in Heaven! The disciples pray to me! Suddenly they are saying to me 'Mother of God'! But who does Mary pray to? Must I now become Mary again, blessed among women. I am afraid, Lord! Why don't You send my angel to me? Don't leave me alone! You know I was afraid when we were making our way back out of Egypt with the child! Herod was dead; all the people who had sought after the child's life were dead; in spite of that I was afraid. Someone would recognise us! The women of Bethlehem – wouldn't they want to be revenged? But they didn't lay a finger on my child, the child who bore the guilt for the death of their children. As if they knew nothing about revenge. And when Your son was following the Way of the Cross and I was standing in the throng of people, and I was nearly collapsing, a woman held me up. She comforted me and said: 'That one there was allowed to live thirty years. My son only got to two years old. King Herod had him murdered.' She didn't know who this Jesus was, but she knew that I was His mother, and she saw that He couldn't be a criminal, like those who were to be crucified with Him. She cried over her child once again, and her tears comforted me.

The shadows are growing longer. The day is drawing to its close. They will be missing me. They will call out for me: 'Miriam! Where is Mary? . . . What will she eat? What will she drink? Is she out of her mind?' It's a good feeling, when you know you'll be missed . . . Now the gentle wind is wafting over the desert. The nightingale has stopped singing. In the distance I can hear the shepherds calling. Soon they will light their fires. This is the same region, but they're different shepherds; they don't know anything; no angel has ever appeared to them. Lord! My feet are sore. There's no water anywhere, for me to cool them. There's no one near to anoint them for me. I am thirsty! It's been a long hot day. My hair is full of sand and my eyes are burning. On the way to Egypt we found a flower that they call the Rose of Jericho. Wherever it blooms there is water. When the water dries up it draws in its roots, then the desert wind sweeps it away. It clenches itself like a fist, and when it finds water again, unfolds like a hand and stretches out its roots once more. Lord! Transform me! Let me become a plant!

The sun has gone down. Are You the sun, Lord? Is Your radiance deserting me? Jesus stayed alone in the desert for forty days and nights, and I have had enough at the end of the first day. The Sabbath is over. In Jerusalem now the streets are filling up with people. I long for my brothers and sisters. I've been separated from them for a whole day now already, an eternity. I think of them as of something far off in the past.

We lived together for tens of years. Our hearts were full of joy! For us every meal became a feast of love. We used to sing as we went about our little chores. Everyone loved each other. No one wanted to keep anything for themselves. 'Take it!' we would say. And nobody said: 'That belongs to me!' My own children didn't say 'Mother' to me any more, they said 'Miriam', or even 'Sister'. When we talked about Jesus, which we did all the time, we called Him: 'He who is risen'; we looked up above towards Him; we looked so hard, by day our rapt gaze pushed the very clouds asunder, by night it parted the constellations in the sky. Whoever was sick was looked after. The old people were cared for by us – we supported them. No one was a burden to us. No one asked: 'Who is responsible?' Anyone who had two pieces of cloth gave one of them to the someone who had none. The men proclaimed our Lord's praise with words, the women sang His praises. We didn't perform any miracles the way the disciples used to, so that people would believe in Him. Women don't need miracles. To us it's miraculous that the sun rises, that fruit grows out of blossoms. Out of a seed-kernel a tree grows, and a human being grows inside us from a man's seed. Before, we had to keep to the house, but now we were free, just the same as the men. We travelled from place to place, people took us in; only a few closed their doors to us.

'Blessed are the peace-lovers,' we said; and 'Blessed are the pure of heart.' Blessed – Father in Heaven, they were blessed times! We had only to utter the name of Jesus and He was with us. 'Do you remember . . . ?' James would say; and he would relate all that had taken place in Capernaus. We talked about Emmaus as if it were only yesterday that Jesus appeared to us there. And Andrew told about the wonderful haul of fish on the Sea of Galilee. We often spend time there on its shores.

Sometimes someone will jump up and call out: 'I will walk across the sea, just like our Lord did!' We hold him back, we assure him that we believe him . . . then he falls back down on the grass, exhausted, as if he'd been walking on the water for hours. Sometimes we join hands and dance. People think that we must be drunk – out of our minds; and we are not in our right minds, not the way other people understand it. We often don't know what we're saying or doing.

When we're in Jerusalem we go to the garden of Gethsemane in the evenings and sit ourselves down under an olive tree and wait for night to fall. Jerusalem lies in darkness, but we keep watch. One of us watches over the others, to make sure that no one drops off to sleep. We grasp each other by the shoulders. 'Wake up!' we shout; 'The cock will be crowing soon!' We hear the nightbirds and the birds that herald the coming of morning. In the first light of the sun we go to the spring and fill our jugs. We pour out the water, and each one gives his cup to the one standing next to him, and the rest of the water we let run all down our faces, pour it over our hands. We feel refreshed and ready for a new day, as if we'd slept for a long time. One person washes another one's feet and anoints them. It's easier to wash other people's feet than your own. Just as it's easier to remove a thorn from the sole of someone else's foot than it is from your own. One person breaks off a piece of bread for the next one. You break off a bigger piece for someone else than for yourself.

Our Father which art in Heaven! Night has closed in around me. But now I'm not afraid any more. Before, Joseph used to have to poke about in the dry grass with his stick to chase away vipers. The great constellations go wheeling on their way up above me. Where to? Where do they come from? The Wise

Men, who came from the East to worship the child, reported that they had seen Your star. Which one is Your star? Aren't all the stars Your stars? Isn't Heaven everywhere after all? Everywhere where it isn't Earth? 'Disciples of the Lord' they call us. And that's their way of mocking us, too. Yes, Lord, they mock us in Your name, because we call ourselves Christians, after Your son Jesus Christ.

What are we to do? They hurl abuse after us. Sometimes they throw stones after us too. Because we annoy them, because we only do whatever is absolutely necessary and we don't follow any regular work. Andrew, who mends our sandals, doesn't make any shoes to sell for money. Hannah mends our garments, but she doesn't sew any new ones. Our clothes are patched, we have a raggedy look. To us that's not important. What's important is to worship and give praise. People don't know that keeping vigil and praying is very exhausting. We are often tired out. We have only the Earth to lie down on to rest, or else we lie on straw. The men let their hair and their beards grow; the women fasten blue flowers of morning glory in their hair to make themselves pleasing to the Lord. We don't own any land or any gardens, that would have to be tilled and harvested. We have no animals to feed and milk and slaughter. So we wander from place to place.

Often we have to beg for our daily bread. We ask for gifts and give thanks for the gifts that we are given in Your name. We live on fish from the Jordan and from the Sea of Galilee. We help ourselves to some of the fruits in the fields, pick grapes in the vineyards – as many as we need, to satisfy our hunger. Sometimes we catch a chicken and have a feast. And then we thank You for Your gifts, that we've helped ourselves to, illegally. It isn't easy to steal. We're not thieves, we haven't learnt the thief's trade. It would be easier to milk a goat and weave a carpet. When my hands, that were used to holding a spindle and spinning, get restless, I play with olive stones that I've threaded on a string.

Lots of people think we're idlers and vagabonds. But there are others who listen to what we say, and a lot join up with us. Mostly it's children that flock around us and want to listen to our stories. When they see us, they shout; 'Tell about the little daughter of Jairus!' The old come to us as well. Those who have not been long on this earth and those who will not be on earth for much longer. They are closer to You. Is that how it is? Father in Heaven! I am speaking out loud, my questions come back to me as echoes, as if You do not hear me. Where do we come from? Where are we going? From You and back to You? It is good to be a child and it is good to be old.

The first years, when we were still overflowing with His nearness and with His spirit; when all we had to do was to speak His name and He was there in our midst – God in Heaven! those years were like one long blessed day. Until then, one day, when first one of the disciples and then another started up, and they said: 'We must pass on what happened! We must write the story of our Lord Jesus Christ down, for those who come after us! We must go to Nazareth and to Cana and to Bethany, and we must ask the neighbours, and the high priests too, in Jerusalem.' And suddenly, suddenly one of them said: 'Well – ask Mary then!' He said Mary and not Miriam, and everyone looked at me and shouted 'Mary! Mary!' And they asked lots of questions and wanted to know what happened all that time ago. They asked about Joseph, my husband. Why did they ask about him?

I told them what I knew: that he came originally from

Nazareth in Galilee, descended from the house and lineage of David. And when the Roman Caesar Augustus – and here, somebody shouted out, right in the middle: 'Cyrenius was Governor in Syria then!' . . . I went on to tell them that he had to be counted in the census – each man in his own city – and so Joseph had to journey to Bethlehem, and because I was pregnant he didn't want to leave me behind all alone. They asked what family was I from. I wasn't counted, I didn't count; but now I had to recount all of it and I wasn't used to recounting. They were very insistent. They asked: 'Did you lay God's son in a pig's trough?' Another one asked: Or in the hay, in a manger, that goats eat from? Was there really an ox standing in the stable? Was it tethered with a rope? They wanted to know how many shepherds came to worship the child, three or four, or was it more? 'You must know, surely!'

I said – and I was crying as I told them, I'd just brought a child into the world, my first, I'd had eyes only for the child, but then – and now I wasn't crying any more – I said: 'I have stored up the angel's words which the shepherd brought me, in my heart.' And I recited the words: 'Fear not, behold, I bring you tidings of great joy.' But of course, my God, You know what the angel said. And once again my sisters and brothers fell down before me, one after the other, and remained on their knees, and it was as if they wanted to worship me and not You. So then I went and stood apart from them.

But on the next day another one came with his writing tablet, and the others sat round him in a circle and they set about interrogating me. They asked me: 'Were you without sin, Mary? Had your husband never lain with you before the Holy Ghost came upon you? You know, God, how it happened, and I said: 'My sisters and brothers, my heart was pure! The angel

135

had appeared to me. For isn't everything without sin that we do in His name? And isn't every child that comes into the world a child of God? After all that's what we've been preaching throughout the whole land! That's what Jesus promised us!'

What a to-ing and fro-ing! They shouted at each other and fought amongst themselves. They talked about sin and pointed at *us*, at the women, who were their sisters – for years we had lived together in love. We women took ourselves off away from them. Father in Heaven we were ashamed, as if we'd been driven out of Paradise a second time. That evening we stayed together. Once again we were divided, men and women. We had found somewhere to put up, in a sheep shed. At night the men banged on the door of the shed and called out our names: 'Hannah! Rebecca! Miriam!' We became restless, like animals that are on heat and cry out.

And on the next morning the men looked at me, and they looked for a long time and they saw in me a woman who has brought children into the world, who has grown old, who gets hungry and thirsty. And I could feel that they had stopped believing. I, Mary, was preventing them from believing. You have not taught me to speak. I am used to listening and to obeying. What else could I have said to them? Together, many times a day we have prayed: 'Lord, Your will be done!' But now that's not enough for them any more, they want to have everything explained, You must needs explain to them why it happened in that way and no other way. They want to know! And yet it is so easy to believe.

The horizon is growing light. As soon as the sun's rays climb above the mountains and I can recognise the path I came on, I shall go back. You have given me no other answer. The wind is caressing my face as if it might be Your hand, blowing away the mist from in front of my eyes. I behold Your glory in the face of the sun. I shall go back and I shall be dumb. They will ask: 'Where did you lose your tongue? You have to speak up as a witness!' But I shall not answer. I have said it all, and You have listened to me.

We have often spoken about our Lord's return. You must needs send Your son down again to earth, over and over again, so that we see with our own eyes what we must believe. Another woman will bring Him into the world, He will perform other miracles in other places, so that we may recognise Your Might. Then it will not be the Jews that persecute Him and crucify Him – others will do it.

Your handmaiden is weary, weary unto death. You know all things, I have spoken to You of the things that You know, and I will not speak to the people about the things they want to know, things that I believe. I am talking like a brook that has been dammed up for a long time. The words gush out, like a fountain. Let me be a rose of Jericho, that withers in the desert, and which the wind drives over the sands and which puts its roots down where there is water.

# *Dead Agamemnon,*

# *are you happy now?*

The unrecorded oration of
Clytaemnestra at the bier
of the King of Mycenae

# Clytaemnestra

*Clytaemnestra was the second daughter of Tyndareus. She was married first to Tantalus (son of Thyestes, not to be confused with the more famous Tantalus, son of Zeus, who was immortalised in the word 'tantalising'). He is said to have been murdered by Agamemnon, king of Argos, who became Clytaemnestra's second husband. Helen, Clytaemnestra's elder sister, was married to Agamemnon's brother Menelaus. Her abduction by Paris sparked off a war with the Trojans. Agamemnon assembled a fleet of one hundred ships, but was unable to set out for Troy for lack of a favourable wind. To appease the goddess Artemis so that she would send a wind Agamemnon sacrificed his eldest daughter Iphigenia. On his return from Troy, after a siege of many years, Clytaemnestra, or her lover, Aegisthus, or both together, murdered him in his bath. She in her turn was murdered by their son Orestes.*

*The remains of Mycenae, including the treasury of Athens and Clytaemnestra's tomb, and the death mask of Agamemnon were first uncovered by the German archaeologist Heinrich Schliemann in the 1870s.*

# Dead Agamemnon,
# are you happy now?

The unrecorded oration of Clytaemnestra
at the bier of the King of Mycenae

Leave me alone with him! He was my husband – what is it you fear for a dead man? That I shall kill him a second time? He would have deserved it.

Agamemnon – you said that in the House of Atreus, there is one choice only: murder or be murdered. I said: 'Good. Murder me! But then I make you a murderer!' Now it has come about the other way around.

You also said: 'Call no man happy until he is dead.' Are you happy now? It's a beautiful morning, this morning, Agamemnon – did you ever see that a morning could be beautiful? Do you know the shadow of the olive tree at midday? Your heralds raise their arms in salute; you are always giving them new slogans to shout out: 'Hail! Victory!' And: 'Zeus Agamemnon!' Why don't they salute you with: 'Good morning!'? If this morning turns out good, that will already be something to be thankful for. I

141

have not known many good days. I have had to seek happiness outside the walls of Mycenae.

I have no feeling of sympathy for you, Agamemnon. Your dog is dead, no dog can live that long. I am not the same woman any more, who used to stand up there on the cliff-top and wait. I hate the sea! I hate standing on the shore staring after ships that sail away and don't come back. And when they come – ten years later is ten years too late.

I stood with my back to the sea when they announced the return of your ships, and saw: Mycenae in ruins, your Liongate burst asunder, and on your tomb, thistles growing. I hated the sea, that is why I drowned you in your bath. Your element is fire, mine is water; you set fire to things, I drown them. I saw the beacons blazing. The heath was on fire on Mount Arachnaion – which they call Spider mountain, did you know that? After all, what do you know of your Argolis? From Mount Ida on Crete, to Mount Hermaeus on Lemnos, to Mount Athos – the flames exchanged their greeting: a relay of fire from mountain top to mountain top. Fire spurted ahead of you. Fire can never be the harbinger of glad tidings.

There you lie, in the great hall of the Palace, stretched out in state on your bier. You never listened to me – listen to me now, listen well, dead Agamemnon! They will argue about whether Aegisthus did this or I. In my heart I have done you to death a hundred times. The intention is what counts, the deed counts for nothing. I am a sponge soaked in hate; and whosoever squeezes that sponge – woe betide him!

When I passed through the Liongate, the lion on the left hand grinned. The stone that I wanted to split you open with – your Lion head – cracked in two, yet the picture remained intact. I get the horrors, Agamemnon! I am not one of those women who say to their husbands: 'Return to me bearing your shield, or else lying dead upon it.' I said to my son Orestes: 'If your shield gets in the way when you run, throw it into the heather.' Orestes, of whom it is said that he wouldn't hurt a fly. Why should he hurt a fly? Later, the Flies will avenge Clytaemnestra.

I asked you to bring me seeds from Troy as booty, seeds of flowers – something that grows. For my gardens; Clytaemnestra's gardens that are now gone wild. Where our children and grandchildren were to play. All I did was conceive these children and give birth to them, they were fed and raised by their wet-nurse. They loved their nurse, not their mother; just as I loved Myrrha, not my mother, Leda. Enmity prevails between Father and Son; and enmity between Mother and Daughter, as it does among the Gods. We have raised enemies, who seek after our lives. The poor care for their own children, because children are the support of their old age.

I have seen so much, Agamemnon, in the alleyways and on the hillsides. For how can you govern a man that you do not know? In any State each man must know each other. He who obeys and he who governs. And every voice must be heard. And there will always be one who speaks softly and one who speaks loud, and many who keep silent. The men meet at the marketplace for no other purpose than to talk. For the Greeks talking is like breathing; to breathe is to talk. Do you want to know who said that? You don't know the man – there isn't a single one you do know! You don't know their women either. They go to the well, or to the river. They talk to each other, but they do their washing and fetch water whilst they talk. The doing and the talking are one. They twitter like birds. But when the King comes they fall silent.

My marriage with you came to an end in that moment when you sacrificed our daughter Iphigenia, all for the sake of a favourable wind. Why didn't you leave my sister Helen in Troy? Does beauty banish guilt? You carried the war over the sea to a distant land, so that your own lands would not be laid waste; your Argolis remained unscathed.

Earthquakes and Wars. Aren't Earthquakes enough? Enough rubble? Enough corpses? The might of the Gods, the might of men! You want to rival the Gods. Battle, glorious Battle! which brings men honour! Explain to me, Agamemnon: what exactly is it that is so very honourable in one man killing the other? He insults the mother who bore him, the father who begot him, the wife who loves him. *Loved* him, Agamemnon! Although you slew my first husband, my first child, I did love you. Guilt breeds guilt. End it! Put an end to it finally, once and for all!

I, Clytaemnestra, sister of the beautiful Helen of Sparta!

I, Clytaemnestra, mother of three daughters and one son!

I, Clytaemnestra, mistress to Aegisthus!

I was not only Agamemnon's wife! So many ways I have tried to tie my name to something of beauty. To a constellation. To my gardens. To a ceremonial cup. But the cup is shattered – the fragments lie mingled in the rubble. Cloudbursts will destroy what is left of my gardens; and the girdle of Clytaemnestra, up there in the heavens, will never be missed.

So – was it senseless to kill Cassandra as well . . . ? Let her live, I said to Aegisthus. Perhaps Orestes will fall in love with Cassandra, they are the same age. He said: You are getting old; you're matchmaking. Perhaps he was taken with her. He always loved whatever you loved. His love is called Vengeance. No one will kill Glaucos, nor Georgios, nor Pavlos; a fisherman, a shepherd, a potter – not worth the death; spared the vengeance of the Gods. The luck of the poor is called obscurity.

You don't have to be called Cassandra to be able to prophesy calamity for the House of Atreus. She must have slept under a hazel bush as a child – that makes your dreams prophetic; I know that from Georgios; Myrrha confirmed it. Cassandra is herself the calamity that she predicts.

If you had come back just one single time without one of your slave-girls in tow! Why do you all build yourselves citadels, when the dwelling you really prefer is the dark belly of some ship? When you would sooner live in a tent? All you need is a Treasury for your booty. Why don't you store your slave-girls in your Treasury? Do you imagine that I had heard nothing about Chryseis, the daughter of the Trojan priest? Nothing about Achilles' favourite slave-girl? Cassandra was the last love, that was why we had to kill her.

For who really wants to know beforehand what is going to happen? No one! Do you hear? I say: No one! That female highwaywoman! Muttering in the backstreets of Mycenae – she'd have gone on like that, churning out curses until in the end what she predicted came to pass: Accursed be this one! Accursed be that one! . . . Orestes will avenge his father, kill his mother! We have stopped her mouth for her.

The moment before sunrise. The moment for murder. A chilly moment for you, I know. Do you want something to cover you? The moment of departure. This is the hour when Glaucos, my fisherman, would bring me back to the shore.

You could only conduct your war because others tilled your fields, gathered in your corn, pressed your grapes, caught your fish, to feed the women and children. Does it surprise you all that other men fathered your children? What is it that counts,

Agamemnon? Say! What counts for you? The countless dead that you have left behind; the sons that you have sired? Any man can get children.

Myrrha says the dead go on hearing what the living are saying, for one hour. So – listen hard! Aegisthus is going to marry our daughter Electra to a farmer. A worthy man. He is already old; he won't produce any descendants. She won't be putting up any claims to Mycenae. But she can claim vengeance. Iphigenia, whom you sacrificed and who was saved by Artemis, serves the goddess now. She was a lamb of patience. But you made of her a sacrificial beast. Gentle Chrysothemis. There is nothing to fear from her – a quiet, cheerful child. You hardly know her. That leaves Orestes. He is nervous. Nervous people are dangerous.

You said that in the House of Atreus there is only one way: to murder or to be murdered; first the one and then the other. Are you still for ever appealing to the will of the Gods? Where is your pride, proud King of Argos? Why don't you say: It was *my* will. I wanted to be revenged . . . I wanted to conquer. I have a lust for battle. I wanted to see the daughter of the King of Troy at my feet! . . . It's not a queen you need at your side – it's slave-girls. And all that was the Will of the Gods? 'The Gods' is the King's name for the King's excuses. And yet all of you say that in War, it's the brave and the strong who fall. Where were you when the Trojans hurled their spears? Who fell in your stead? How is it that you have come back?

What will remain of you now? Two handfuls of ashes. Fragments. Your Lion Gate. Agamemnon's grave. You want immortality. But I want death. I want to be forgotten. No one should ever speak the name Clytaemnestra. In Argos, when

146

transgressors are pardoned, their brows are crowned with laurel. I used to lay a sprig of laurel on your couch; you were meant to know that I was initiated now, and that I had pardoned you. I used a whole grove of laurels up for you!

Remember! I decorated your spear with jasmine blossoms, so that it wouldn't catch the first rays of sunlight and waken you. You were late setting out; when you emerged from my chamber with your flower-bedecked wand, how they laughed! It was not often that anyone laughed in Argos.

What am I to do? What do your Gods require? Suicide? Remorse? But remorse for what? Because you slew my first husband, when I was still young? My first child? Just because you took Iphigenia from me – for that? Because you went away for ten years? What use to you was faithfulness in a wife who doesn't love you? We will not lie side by side together in one grave. It's Cassandra whom they should lay at your feet, the beauteous spoil of Troy.

That was what you liked: firm little breasts, slender feet, shapely arms. And are you beautiful, ancient Agamemnon? Your belly sags, your neck has run to fat, you drag your legs, your arms dangle feebly. You wore splints on your legs because they were crooked. Did you think I didn't know? I didn't notice at once; but when I did, I didn't stop loving my husband; not yet. I ask, what woman can say of herself that she has never thought of murder – that she has never dreamed of murder? I say she lies! I thought of murder a hundred times before you made me a murderess. The guilt is yours.

When I entered into marriage with you, I burned the gall of a sacrificial beast, so that we could live together without anger. I burned the spindle that I used to play with in Crete; I cut off my curls and burned them. But my gall filled up again

147

with rage. My curls grew back! My looking-glass — that is me! My Me — who belongs to me. You took my looking-glass away from me when you set out for Troy. No looking-glass, no love? Another man gave me another mirror.

My face is naked — you have never seen me like this. A queen is expected to wear paint and powder, so that she never shows her real face. Unless her family is in mourning. The House of Atreus is always in mourning. Now I will paint my face, Agamemnon! As a sign that I do not mourn you. I will bind my bosom to lift up my breasts, and I will pick out the dress I wore as a girl, slit up to here; it shows my legs right to the knee. I have grown fat.

You have never seen me cry, ancient son of Atreus? Now you see my tears. I am crying for myself. You cannot close your eyes for yourself any more. Look! Look! A time will come when women will rebel; then they won't be expected any more to stay young and beautiful. It is not a virtue; it's not an achievement.

Aegisthus should have abducted me, the way Paris abducted my sister Helen. Wasn't I beautiful enough? Wasn't I worth a war? 'As beautiful as Helen' that's what they used to say, throughout the whole country. Menelaus is taking her back. She is damaged goods. But for her, I should have been the fairest in Sparta. Aegisthus is after your land, he isn't after me. He's after Mycenae, Tiryns, Argos — your cities; he wants your pine forests — he needs the wood for new ships, new wars. What am I to do? Ask the Gods? But of course they don't talk with women — according to you men! I prayed for the winds to die down, so that your ships would not reach Troy. Myrrha says that my prayer was half-hearted. Should I go to Georgios, who was my lover? Should I look after the goats with him? I would soon be found. They need me as witness.

The glorious hero Agamemnon, with his incendiary eyes! Who is to close your eyelids for you? Cassandra is dead. Your daughter Electra? Or me? When I used to dream about you – yes, you hear aright, I have dreamed of you – you were carrying your spear. Both your spears, do you remember? When you wanted to use one of them you put the other away. One in the evening, the next morning the other one – oh yes! Agamemnon, yes! Now they both lie still.

You had to be drowned before you would listen to me. Before you found time for Clytaemnestra. I am giving your funeral oration, listen carefully! Zeus himself decides on the outcome of a war. Did you forget that, haughty king of Mycenae? What a humiliation for a man so hungry for power! You are merely an instrument. So why are they all accusing me? I have only done what your Gods wanted!

I cannot wait. I am not the stuff widows are made of. I wept, as long as my tears lasted, at the possibility of your death. Now you are an old man. I felt no pity when I saw you again. Cassandra was in the same chariot, seated at your feet, cursing away. Your bed didn't stand empty for ten years. It's cold within the walls of Mycenae.

As soon as the sun climbs above the hill they will put your mask on for you. Do you remember the goldsmith? He sat in front of you for a long time, gazing into you; he saw into the future. He made you visible to all. I was to keep the mask for you, until your return; until your death. I often used to hold it in my lap and speak with you. As I am speaking with you now. You didn't have a beard in those days. Wasn't there a barber in Troy? Did you want to please Priam's daughter?

Did you not want her to see your fat chin? Your ears stick out
– that comes from eavesdropping. Eavesdroppers are always
full of fear – it makes their ears grow. That's what Georgios the
shepherd says.

Your tomb stands in readiness – a giant's cavern. Everything
you men have built is too big for humans. You had walls erected
that were fit for the Cyclops. Was it to stop the screams from
piercing them – my screams – that you had the walls of Tiryns
and Mycenae built so strong? The sun never lights up the halls,
never warms them. Do you feel cold, Agamemnon? You often
used to brag: I am made out of bronze, you boasted. Good –
then rust! Even rust decays.

I want to turn into Earth. No portrait of Clytaemnestra, no
mask. Only a rumour, a shadow lying over Mycenae. You are
little, Agamemnon; did you know that you are so little? You will
be frightened inside your great tomb, which looks like a phallus.
Do you imagine no one would recognise the phallus in which
you will soon be sitting prisoner? There is grass growing on the
hillside – I was there only yesterday. Poppies are in bloom, and
camomile, too. People will walk about over you. Bats will make
their homes in your tomb. Isn't that what Cassandra prophesied
for you? Rats and mice? Later on the shepherds will seek refuge
in your burial chamber. It will make their flesh creep, but then
the sheep and goats will push through the doorway, their greasy
pelts will rub against the walls until they make them gleam.
They will shit all over you, Agamemnon! The shepherds will
light fires against the darkness and the cold. Smoke will blacken
the stones. And your mask will be found only beneath layers of
dust and dung.

What are your Gods planning for Clytaemnestra? Will she

be hurled into the sea from the cliff-top? Struck by lightning? Will fish eat away my flesh; or will vultures pick it from my bones? My lips? My eyes? Slowworms encircle my arms? When I was still young you gave me a present of a bangle in the form of a snake, with eyes of ruby red. The bangle lies on the bottom of the sea, not far from the cliff where I used to stand and wait. No one will eat the fish they catch there – poisoned by Clytaemnestra's flesh. My hatred poisons Argos. Will wild bees forbid the entrance to my grave? Will the honeycomb be torn from the children's hands? 'You mustn't eat that, the honey is bitter, you will die, Clytaemnestra's hatred has poisoned it!' What else was it Cassandra said? Where Hatred and Destruction rule, they will speak of Chaos – of that little river Chaos, whose bed I often crossed; it will be choked with rubble. Zeus will destroy with lightning; Poseidon will make the earth shake. Mycenae in flames and in ruins.

I shall tell Myrrha that they should lay me with my face to the ground, back to Gaia, the Earth mother, who is compassionate. Only when we are both dead, Agamemnon, murdered and murderess, only then shall we be even.

Now it is getting light. Dawn is heralded by the Sun.

Wear your mask, Agamemnon. I am wearing mine.